Contents

CONTENTS

Introduction

The position of music in the secondary school curriculum has been under increasing scrutiny during the past few years. Whilst extra-curricular music has continued to flourish, as shown, for example, in the Schools' Prom, the state of music within the curriculum seems to be less healthy. It has been recognized that if music is to have a place in schools, it must become relevant to all pupils as suggested recently in *Curriculum Matters 4: Music from 5-16* (HMSO). In this booklet, as in the GCSE criteria, composing has been given a new importance, alongside listening and performing. These three areas should be included and interlinked in a practical course of music education.

Composing is not, nor can it be, an excuse or a vehicle for 'self-expression', yet musical experience is intensely emotional, expressive, personal, and powerful. Suzanne Langer, in *Feeling and Form*, describes music not as self-expression, but as the 'formulation and representation of emotions, moods, mental tensions and resolutions—a "logical picture" of sentient, responsive life, a source of insight, not a plea for sympathy.' The emotional power of music is undeniable, yet some forms of curriculum practice seem to substitute for musical experience the study of music. Such study may be appropriate for the musicologist, but not for secondary schooling. Music is a powerful medium, and this power must not be avoided in education.

There are those who maintain that musical patterns have no relation to human emotions; and that our appreciation of music is purely aesthetic. In this view, music has no meaning outside itself, and the listener's enjoyment of a musical work is the consequence of his appreciation of its structure. Of course the appreciation of musical form is a vital aspect of musical appreciation in general; but it is impossible to accept that this constitutes the whole of our response. Music generates emotion; in fact, a whole range of physiological responses which can be measured, including changes in pulse-rate, blood pressure, rate of respiration, muscular energy. Any consideration of music which pays attention only to aesthetic form, and which omits to take into account its emotional content, must be ruled out of court.'

A. Storr, *The Dynamics of Creation*

Unless music in education is based firmly upon first-hand practical experience the education offered will be only 'about' music, not of it. If music is to justify its existence as a curriculum subject it must offer something unique and valuable. It must make a contribution to the development of the individual in a way that no other subject can. This can occur through musical expression developing from personal experience, which can help the individual towards an understanding of himself, and of himself in relation to other people. A reverence for the past at the expense of the present is as reprehensible an attitude as one which ignores the richness of a musical heritage spanning several centuries and many cultures.

It is possible to allow education to proceed in this way, to step out of the bounds of teaching only 'about' music, without resorting to an unstructured 'free for all' with little discernible progress from week to week. Such a style of education I call 'Music in a Creative Education', implying a scheme in which 'creative' musical statements—statements original to the individual—are made, but within the context of a very firm structure, and in a planned curriculum which gradually leads the individual forward in terms of expressive potential, sensitivity, musical awareness, self-awareness.

The courses described in this book all attempt, in varying degrees, to relate musical expression to areas of experience that children have already encountered, or are likely to encounter, in everyday life. It is important not only that people have something to say, but also that they have the means of saying it. Thus the subjects chosen for the different courses can generate powerful feelings through which purely 'musical' lessons can be learnt—lessons concerning structure, balance, contrast, texture, melody, rhythm, instrumental colour, and so on—and at the same time open the door to the 'inner' world of imagination, awareness, sensitivity, feelings, identity. Having such awareness, and the ability to give expression to it via the abstract medium of music, can be very liberating—out of bounds!

The scope of the course

The schemes of work which follow are designed for the first three years of the secondary school—for pupils aged 11 to 13 (although they may be easily adapted for both younger and older pupils). It is important for children of this age to have something concrete to 'hang on to', so the music created on these courses is always 'about' something. The expression is not always solely through the medium of music, although this is always of paramount importance. The artificial boundaries of the curriculum and timetable do not always encourage a combination of the expressive arts, but this work tends to lead towards such a combination. Thus wherever possible it would be most useful if these courses could be run in tandem with the art department. If this is not possible, try to have access to basic art department equipment—large sheets of sugar paper, coloured pens, pencils, paint, etc. It is likely that expression will be realized in a variety of forms—music, music with dance, mime, theatre, projection, words—or in various combinations of them.

Following the conclusion of a piece of work, there are often occasions when music of the past can be experienced creatively—as something valuable. If groups have worked in a particular area it is only natural to listen to the work of others who have explored a similar theme. Having worked in the area and been involved in expression, individuals can often find a great deal in subsequently listening to other musics: an involved concentration often leads to active appreciation.

Course structure

It is vital that everyone feels secure and knows exactly what is required. Only then can truly expressive, creative work be possible. Each course lasts for a complete term, occasionally longer, and structure is given by a worksheet, usually a homework sheet. This directs pupils to various tasks associated with the topic. These are researched over a number of weeks so that a body of information—often very stimulating in its own right—is gradually built up.

The printed instructions on the worksheets have deliberately been kept to a minimum, as too much written information/instruction can easily discourage the pupil. It is always more beneficial to talk and discuss ideas rather than issue printed instructions, and this activity forms an important part of the Key lessons, of which there may be two or more on any course.

Key lessons

These are crucial to the success of the course, and each course begins with at least one Key lesson, given with the whole class. The first Key lesson is spent in giving a general introduction to the course: the scope of practical work for the whole term—including mixed-media possibilities—can be outlined. The most important part of the lesson, having distributed the homework sheet (or worksheet), is a discussion of the research to be done. With care, a lively interest can be stimulated through discussion, and it is very important to create enthusiasm for the subject of the course during this lesson.

The research done for homework can often result in beautifully presented books or folders of work. Exercise books seem best for first-year pupils; loose folders and paper can be more appropriate for older pupils. Each pupil will work according to his/her ability, and some will produce a surprising amount. Weekly or fortnightly checks are obviously important, and such checks can provide interesting material for class discussion. This will lead to further stimulation and positive feedback, both important aspects of this kind of education.

Much of the information discovered through homework will be useful in the latter part of the course, and because time is needed for this work to be done, most of the courses are in two parts: an introductory period during which small-scale pieces can be made, usually using only the medium of sound; and a second stage during which information discovered from homework can be used. This can often result in ambitious mixed-media work.

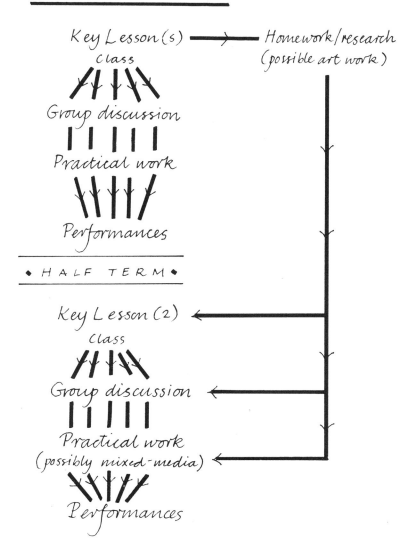

A continuation of the first Key lesson would consider the first piece of **practical work**. There are usually a few possible starting points and these can be discussed with the whole class. Following this, the class would divide into a number of small groups—between four and eight per group—and discuss and plan their first piece of work. This stage is crucial, as several decisions have to be made by each group: 'What is the piece about (i.e., what are we trying to say)?' 'How will we organize it (structure)?' 'What instruments do we want?' 'Who is going to play what?' It is important that such decisions should be made *before* practical work is attempted, so that potential arguments are avoided, such as 'Who is playing the cymbal, glockenspiel, organ, etc. this time?' It is worthwhile for a written plan containing this information to be produced by each group. Although changes will be made during practical work as ideas develop, a written plan can act as a useful focus.

Practical guidelines

Although it is possible for several groups to work at their chosen piece together, it is far better if a place can be found where each group can work in relative privacy. Corridors, cloakrooms, empty classrooms, stock cupboards, and practice rooms (if you're lucky enough to have any) can be useful places to send groups to, and the following few weeks would be spent by groups working out and rehearsing their pieces.

During this time the teacher would spend each lesson visiting each group periodically—not too often—to listen to work in progress, discuss ideas and problems, and offer help and encouragement where necessary.

There is a fear that pupils will only 'mess about' if given unsupervised freedom. This can happen, of course, but if all groups know what they are trying to do, have an idea of how to achieve their aims, and also know when performances will be required, the resulting high degree of self-motivation should dispense with most 'discipline' problems. Any problems can usually be traced back to confusion on the part of the individual, which can normally be resolved through discussion. In this style of working, any individual not contributing to the work, or one being 'difficult', is often dealt with by the other people in the group. They do not take kindly to being prevented from working as they wish, and disruptive elements can become very unpopular!

Performance

When groups are ready—and if the timing is carefully managed—performances of the initial piece of the course can take place in the final week of the first half of term. At these sessions, each group in turn would perform to the rest of the class. It seems very useful to tape-record each performance. This encourages absolute quiet on the part of the audience (who will stifle coughs and sneezes), as well as intense concentration and a real desire to 'get it right this time' on the part of the performers.

Following the group performances the different pieces can be discussed and sections re-heard from the tape. This can be particularly valuable, as the most effective passages can be identified and the techniques used discussed. This part of the lesson can contribute towards further progress and development, helping groups to become more confident and successful in the future. It is illuminating to observe the concentration whole classes often show when listening to performances, and they will often ask to re-hear the complete tape.

At this stage it can be useful to play some music which has been written on a similar theme and to encourage critical listening. Questions such as, 'Is it successful?' ('If so how/If not, why not?'), and 'What do you particularly like/dislike about the piece?' can be considered, and answers jotted down during the playing of a record to provide the subject for discussion. Further playings of the piece can act as a stimulus for creative writing or drawing, and many sensitive poems can result from this activity, which can be of use in the second part of the course. It does seem very helpful to give some task to a class when music is played for a class to listen to; a physical, expressive response to music acts as a focus and is particularly important as an aid to extended concentration to pupils of this age-range. If the choice of

a write a poem or story;

b draw a picture or abstract pattern to show your response to the music; or

c sit down/lie down with eyes shut and listen is given to a class, a large majority will choose from **a** and **b** above. This can lead to repeated hearings, and some may well ask to continue this in their own time! Appreciation can grow and develop as a result of experience.

This sequence of **Key lesson**, **Practical**, **Performance** would be repeated in the second half of the term. In this part of the course the most ambitious work would be produced, including some mixed-media pieces. Some groups may well come up with ideas which are not on the worksheet and these are obviously to be encouraged if suitable and possible, as maximum motivation is achieved if a group devises its own course of work entirely!

Equipment/resources

For research purposes the school library is the best source. Often classes may have a 'library lesson' on their timetable, a lesson in which they use the library for reading or other work. By arrangement some research may well be possible in this time, the librarian being the best person available to direct pupils to relevant material.

School textbooks on a variety of subjects can be useful on many courses, and much other useful material—posters, slides, film strips—can often be borrowed and exploited.

The local town library can be a valuable asset. Given sufficient warning, if the subject-matter and age-range of pupil is given, this library will often assemble a box full of books, etc., which can be borrowed for a complete term. This provides a very useful and easy way of obtaining a wide range of suitable source material. Other relevant sources for specific subjects are given at the end of each chapter.

For practical work, a wide range of classroom percussion instruments will provide the basic sound sources. A variety of other instruments is helpful, and could include orchestral instruments and instruments of non-Western origin. Old pianos can be obtained free of charge, and if they are dismantled to leave only the frame and soundboard, these can be a very valuable sound source, providing a wide variety of sounds and always capturing the interest of pupils.

The use of tape-recorders is highly recommended. The benefits of this piece of equipment are significant, and ideally every group should have a tape-recorder as a standard piece of equipment for each piece, although it is quite possible to work these courses without such a facility. The most obvious benefits are:

a By having a tape-recorder and their own spool of tape or cassette, groups can gradually, week by week, build up quite lengthy pieces of work and can rehearse and record the best possible performance.

b Being able to record their work, groups can then stand back and listen to it far more objectively than would otherwise be possible. This enables constructive criticism to be a positive part of the process, and continuing development is more likely.

c If three-speed tape-recorders can be provided, they can be used to transform sounds—speeding sound up or slowing it down will capture the imagination and extend the expressive potential significantly. Such equipment can be viewed as the equivalent of musical microscopes of great power, both aurally and expressively.

Other useful items of equipment which will change a live sound into something potentially more exciting and interesting include reverberation, echo, delay line, phaser, flanger, filter, etc. Most of these sound units are readily available from music or guitar shops, and many pupils may already possess some. They will all accept a microphone input so that any sound can be transformed and extended. Ideally each group would have a tape recorder and one such device, as well as a variety of percussion instruments. Standard orchestral instruments can also be useful, and the 'traditional' instrumentalist can make very useful contributions to group work.

Many pupils may have one of the many cheap electronic keyboard instruments which have come on the market in the past few years. These are also most useful, producing a variety of different sounds, and many allow some sounds to be created by the player.

Ideally some synthesizers should also be available. These enable virtually any sound to be created, and some also allow external sounds to be input so that different treatments can be given.

It seems best to organize the music room so that practical work is easily possible—instruments can be collected and returned with a minimum of difficulty and performances can be given effectively. I organized the music room as shown in the diagram.

Groups could thus see what instruments were available and collect them and return them on their way in or out of the room; as each instrument had its place it was easy to check that all equipment had in fact been returned. Desks were not needed, and by arranging classes in a circle around the edge of the room the performance area was maximized, and class/group discussion easily and effectively organized.

If tape recorders and other electric/electronic equipment is available, it is a good idea to have a number of trollies. These can always have a tape-recorder and microphone set up on them, and groups can thus transport this equipment, and other instruments, around the school easily and safely.

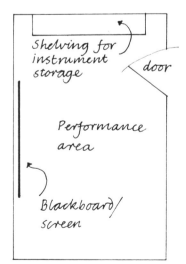

Patterns

Aims To generate musical ideas from various types of pattern and also explore the connection between sound and various types of symbol.

Equipment Access to art department equipment (sugar paper, coloured pens, pencils, etc). Classroom percussion instruments, cassette tape-recorders and (at least) one three-speed tape-recorder.

Structure This course is ideal for first-year pupils during either the first or the second term. It lasts for one complete term and is in two sections, so that with careful planning the half-term holiday will form a natural break.

KEY LESSON 1 ## *Bells and Morse Code*

Bells The worksheet should be distributed (see pages 15–16) and an explanation of the first two sections, 'Bells' and 'Morse Code', then occupies the lesson. The next few weeks' work will be based on these two subjects, the rest of the worksheet being dealt with in the second Key lesson. It is worth reading the text of the worksheet aloud to the class, even though they will all have a copy! Then the sequence of events for 'Bells' can be explored in more detail, as follows:

Practical work

a Divide the whole class into four groups and place these towards the four corners of the music room. Each group should have a number: 1, 2, 3, 4. Starting with the first column of numbers on the worksheet, each group chants its number out loud in the printed sequence. It is helpful at this stage to point to the group whose turn it is to say its number. Initially this will be quite slow, but gradually greater speed can be attained, and it might eventually be possible to stop 'conducting' the exercise.

b When the class can manage the first stage reasonably well each group should decide on one vocal sound to make in place of saying its number. If such sounds are comical, so much the better. An accurate, fairly quick performance of one of the printed columns from the worksheet should then be worked at—this may take some time!

c Have a selection of different classroom percussion instruments available. Make one sound on each and get, through discussion, ideas from the class as to how it can be represented as a shape and a colour. For example, a fairly loud bang on a bass drum is a dark and heavy sound. To represent this on paper a dark colour—brown or black perhaps—can be used, perhaps in a raggedly circular shape.

A triangle, however, is a bright sound, much more delicate and quiet. A triangular shape indicating the natural decay of the sound and a bright but delicate colour, yellow or pink perhaps, can be used to represent this sound.

Glockenspiels, xylophones, claves, maracas, recorders, melodicas, tambourines, etc., can be similarly discussed and some examples shown to the whole class. This is particularly effective if shapes are drawn in colour using an overhead projector. Following this, groups can draw quite interesting 'sound scores' which can be played using the instruments specified. These can also serve as colourful decoration for the music-room walls (as on page 14).

d Groups wishing to work at this area of the worksheet for the next few weeks would then:

1 Make up their own sequence of numbers (having used that on the worksheet for practice purposes) or find a sequence used by bell-ringers. It is worth stressing that a sequence using more than numbers 1–6 can become too complex for pupils of this age to handle.

2 Having practised their own number sequence, each person in the group saying the correct number in turn, instruments should then be chosen, one for each number in the sequence. The group should then practise performing their number sequence until an accurate performance can be given.

3 An accurate score should then be prepared by the group on large paper—sugar paper and felt-tip pens are ideal for this. As each number has become an instrumental sound, and each instrumental sound can be represented as a shape with its own colour, very attractive and decorative scores can be produced.

The final stage is a performance of the piece to the rest of the class, complete with an accurate score.

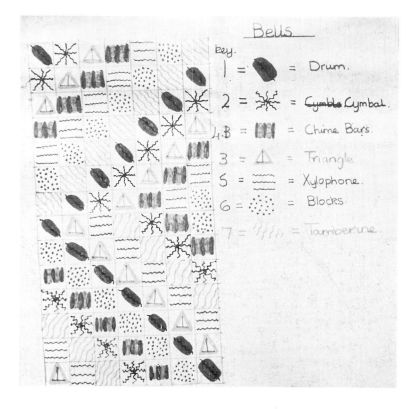

Morse code

The other piece which can be worked is based on morse code. It is likely that the 'Bells' explanation will take at least one full lesson, so that 'Morse Code' may well have to be explained in the following lesson.

Practical work

It is, again, worth reading the text of this section of the worksheet to the whole class first. Having done this, the explanation can take the following form:

a Explain that a dot is a short sound and a dash a long sound. (This may seem obvious, but it is surprising how necessary such explanations seem to be!) It is then worth demonstrating how to make short sounds on naturally sustaining percussion instruments like glockenspiels, cymbals, triangles, etc., and also how to make non-sustaining percussion instruments like drums, xylophones, claves, etc., produce continuous sounds by means of tremolo.

b Only two symbols are used in morse code: a dot (·) and a dash (–). Therefore, any group attempting this starting point should choose up to four different instruments and decide on four different colours. (This exercise tends to be too complex if more than four are used.)

c A *short* phrase should be chosen and converted into morse code. Again it is worth doing this on an overhead projector so that the class can *see* how it is done. It is then possible, using different colours, to show how simple canons are possible; how to write retrograde versions; how to split the parts up between the sequence of dots and dashes; and so on. If two or three different parts are written up fairly quickly the class can be divided into the appropriate number of groups and some attempts at performance made. If the 'text' is amusing—'I hate school' is quite a popular choice!—a useful enthusiasm for accurate performance can be created.

Having had both 'Bells' and 'Morse Code' carefully explained to them, each group will be in a position to choose which of these areas they will work. Whichever area they choose, each group, at the time of performance, will play their piece and also have an accurate score. If performances are timed for half-term the second key lesson can provide the first lesson after the holiday.

The Lazy Dog

13

Patterns Worksheet

Bells

Bell-ringers use patterns of numbers when ringing quite complicated changes. Here is a simple pattern using only four numbers:

1234	1324	4321
2341	4132	1432
3412	2413	2143
4123	3241	3214
1432	1423	4123
4321	4231	3412
3214	2413	2341
2143	3142	1234

By substituting a musical sound for each number quite interesting patterns can be constructed. Make up a number pattern of your own, or find a sequence used by bell-ringers. Construct a piece of music based on your pattern and then write this down again using appropriate shapes and colours instead of numbers to show which instruments are playing.

Morse code

Morse code was invented by S. F. D. Morse (1791–1872) and is a system of signalling by a code in which each letter of the alphabet is represented by a combination of dots and dashes. See if you can use this system to invent interesting patterns (messages) and perform them as pieces of music. Write down your piece using colour to distinguish between the different instruments you use.

A	· –	J	· – – –	S	· · ·	full stop	· · · · · ·	7	– – · · ·
B	– · · ·	K	– · –	T	–	comma	– – · · – –	8	– – – · ·
C	– · – ·	L	· – · ·	U	· · –	1	· – – – –	9	– – – – ·
D	– · ·	M	– –	V	· · · –	2	· · – – –	0	– – – – –
E	·	N	– ·	W	· – –	3	· · · – –		
F	· · – ·	O	– – –	X	– · · –	4	· · · · –		
G	– – ·	P	· – – ·	Y	– · – –	5	· · · · ·		
H	· · · ·	Q	– – · –	Z	– – · ·	6	– · · · ·		
I	· ·	R	· – ·						

Constellations

For centuries man has recognized patterns of stars in the sky. Some of these star patterns are better known than others, the signs of the zodiac being perhaps the most familiar:

Cancer (the crab)
Leo (the lion)
Virgo (the virgin)
Libra (the scales)
Scorpio (the scorpion)
Sagittarius (the archer)
Capricornus (the goat)
Aquarius (the water-carrier)
Pisces (the fish)
Aries (the ram)
Gemini (the twins)
Taurus (the bull)

Other well-known constellations include the Plough, Pegasus, Orion and Hercules.

Choose at least one constellation and find out as much as you can about it. Draw the shape of the stars and the animal or other being associated with it.

Clocks

Alarm; church; grandfather; Big Ben; chimes; pendulum . . .

Clocks make regular patterns of sound, move in regular ways at constant speeds . . .

Take the idea of CLOCKS and use it in any way you can to produce a piece of music (and mime if you wish).

Machines

Take a cassette tape-recorder and record as many mechanical sounds as you can from the environment: cars, lorries, cement-mixers, clocks, typewriters, washing machines, lathes, drills, and so on.

Having recorded many different patterns of sound, construct a piece of music on tape using different speeds to make different effects.

Games

Bring in a pack of playing-cards. Select a suitable number of cards from the pack. Decide what each suit is to mean, and also what the numbers represent. (Hearts could be xylophone, spades drums; high numbers could mean loud sounds, low numbers soft; the number could mean how many sounds are to be made, or whereabouts in the room sounds should be made; etc.)

Experiment with different ideas and try to make up a game which can be played with about four people using four different instruments.

Invent a musical game of your own. This could consist of designing a pack of 'musical' cards with rules, or you may invent a 'board' game using snakes and ladders, ludo, etc., as a model. Design and make your game. Write out the rules so that others can play too.

KEY LESSON 2 *Constellations, clocks, machines and games*

The second part of this course allows far greater freedom of choice, and this Key lesson is taken up with a description of how the remaining starting-points from the worksheet can be used.

Constellations

Many pupils will be familiar with their own star signs as a large proportion will regularly read their horoscope in magazines or newspapers. The school library will have books which contain the pattern of stars which represents each star sign, and some discussion of the supposed characteristics of people with a certain star sign can be useful.

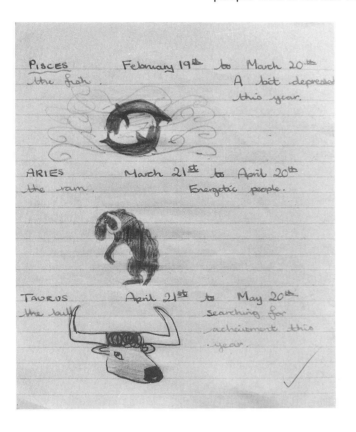

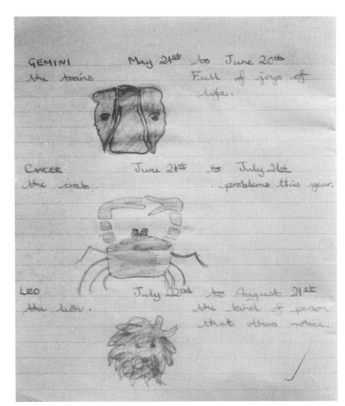

Practical work

There are several ways of using this information to generate musical ideas:

a   A score can be produced consisting of a number of star patterns drawn on paper in different colours. Each colour represents a different instrument. The group has to make decisions concerning speed, dynamics, pitch, etc., in order to devise the most effective performance.

b   The different characteristics of various people born under different star signs—thoughtful, lively, unstable, etc.—can become a feature of the music. A group could thus produce a small suite of movements representing their own star signs.

c   The animals or other beings with which the star signs are associated can act as a focus for different pieces. Thus music for LEO would be strong and majestic, whereas that for PISCES would be more gentle and wavy.

17

Music-theatre can become an extra form of expression, particularly in (**b**) and (**c**), with groups making costumes to personify the characteristics being explored in the music. Mimes and dance can thus be developed to accompany the music.

Clocks

Regular rhythms and ostinato figures tend to feature strongly in pieces constructed on this theme. Many imitations of musical clocks—different chimes for the quarter, half, three-quarter, and hour—are possible, some using percussion instruments, others using voices. Pupils can usefully be directed to think about structure in this piece, rondo being a suitable form for the repetition which is present in chiming clocks. The 'Viennese Musical Clock' from Kodály's *Háry János* is a clear example of such a structure. Groups working the theme using only voices may find part of Patterson's *Time Piece* quite stimulating.

Practical work

This particular area is excellent for some sort of music-theatre. Because of the mechanical regularity of clocks very successful mimes can be constructed to accompany such work. Some groups using only voices may perform the piece in music and movement, the different members of the group becoming different parts of the clock. The piece may start with the clock being wound up, running for a while and chiming occasionally, then gradually running down and grinding to a halt. This gives a most effective structure to the music, resembling an arch form.

Some groups who use instruments for their music may care to make a tape of their performance and produce a mime to go with the tape, or to combine some additional sounds performed live with the tape. Such pieces often begin as above, with the clock being wound up, running and chiming normally for a time, but gradually going wrong and ending with a violent explosion and the different parts of the clock being scattered far and wide. Again, this provides a very satisfactory structure in purely musical terms.

Machines Practical work

This is technically the most complex of all the pieces of the PATTERNS course and it demands a great deal of time and commitment from any group which chooses to work it. They have to be willing to put in extra work, outside class time, in order to complete it (generally), and so I tended to limit this piece to one group in any class. The piece is in three stages:

a Using a portable cassette recorder (with batteries and built-in microphone), the group visits various locations around the school and records mechanical sounds—woodwork/metalwork areas, typing room, domestic science, etc. If possible, a visit to a nearby railway station or bus park can also be fruitful. These sounds are then transferred to reel-to-reel tape, being recorded at the 'middle' speed. ('Slow', 'middle', and 'fast' in this context refer to tape speeds 4.8, 9.5, and 19 cms per second, respectively.)

b Three columns are drawn on paper. These are labelled either 'slow', 'middle', or 'fast'. With the tape counter set at zero, the tape is first of all played back at the middle speed. In the column labelled 'middle' each sound should be listed, together with its position on tape—i.e. the number on the tape counter when the sound begins. Having worked the complete tape in this way it should then be rewound and the procedure repeated for the other two speeds. When playing back the tape at 'slow' or 'fast', the effect of the speed change should be noted: some will be very interesting; others less so.

c A selection of all the available sounds has to be made. Some will no doubt be at the original speed, but many will be at either the 'slow' or the 'fast' speed. Having chosen the most interesting and effective sounds, these have then to be placed in a satisfactory order. (Contrasts of speed, pitch, dynamic, etc., are important considerations at this stage.)

Once an order is decided, the relevant sounds may be re-recorded on to another cassette. The cassette can be stopped after each sound while the next sound is found and the appropriate speed selected. Interesting results can be achieved when the final cassette is replayed. Although the quality will not be of a high standard, it represents a considerable achievement for first-year pupils who are unlikely to have used such equipment in this way before. Groups who have completed this piece may be interested in hearing some 'electronic' music. Part of Subotnik's *Silver Apples of the Moon* is very accessible to pupils of this age, particularly the first few minutes of side two.

Games *Practical work*

This section is in two parts:

a The instructions on the worksheet should be clear enough for groups to proceed. The use of playing cards is only to give groups an idea of some of the possibilities, and it is best to spend only a short time trying out ideas in this section.

b Ideas for board games can be taken from snakes and ladders, ludo, cluedo, etc. From them, quite complex musical games can be devised. Groups have to produce their own board, any cards and counters which may be necessary, and also a set of rules. This area in particular seems to capture the interest, and usually many very interesting games are produced.

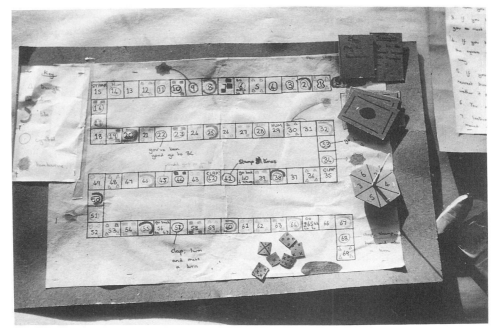

A follow-up to this assignment could be the introduction of David Bedford's two 'game' pieces, either for the group to try out, or for the whole class to use—after the completion of the course. These are *An Exciting Game for Children of All Ages* and *Fun for All the Family*. Occasionally a group will devise a game piece which the whole class can play, and this can be a most successful way of ending the term!

Other starting points

The list of possible starting points on the worksheet can easily be extended, and some groups may have other ideas for developing pieces out of the idea of PATTERNS (using patterned material or wallpaper as musical scores and then designing their own wallpaper for decorative and performance purposes, for example). However, the second Key lesson should give enough variety of starting points for every group to be able to find something of interest to work at for the remainder of the term.

Results

It is unlikely that any group would complete more than one piece in the second half of the term, but at the end of this course each group should have produced two pieces, each with an accurate accompanying score (apart from the 'Machines' group), and such pieces can of course be performed by other classes and groups.

Resources

Kodály: *Háry János*
Patterson: *Time Piece*
Subotnik: *Silver Apples of the Moon*

Other music for performance

Bedford: *An Exciting Game for Children of All Ages*   Universal Edition
Bedford: *Fun for All the Family*   Universal Edition

Supernatural

Aims   To introduce the idea of music-theatre and mixed-media forms of expression. Some simple electronic devices can be introduced through practical work.

Equipment   Three-speed tape-recorders; echo and reverberation devices.
Access to art department equipment (sugar paper, paints, felt tip pens, etc.).
Slide projectors.

Structure   This is an ideal course with which to finish the year. It always seems to capture the imagination, and new equipment and techniques can be introduced. It is in two parts, the mid-term holiday providing a natural break.

KEY LESSON 1   ## *Introducing the supernatural*

This lesson is in two sections, research and practical.

Research   The homework sheet (see page 22) should be distributed and discussed. Although it is very straightforward, it is worth talking about various superstitions and supposed supernatural happenings: 'What is so unlucky about the number 13?' 'Why say "bless you" when someone sneezes?' 'Why throw salt over your shoulder if you spill some?' 'Why not walk under a ladder?' 'Has anyone seen a ghost, or does anyone know of somebody who has?'—and so on. Quite lively discussion can result from this, and although there should be considerable natural interest in the subject, such discussion at this stage can create considerable enthusiasm for homework!

Notes to the homework sheet

a   Word definitions: one or two sentences per word is a minimum target.

b   An imaginative story or poem: this can be written at home or in class time. During this course there are one or two pieces of music which can be played to the complete class as an inspiration for effective writing (see **Resources**, below).

c   This section can be an opportunity for individuals or groups to interview a number of people and either write down the results of the interview, or record

Supernatural Homework sheet

a Find out as much as you can about the following:

supernatural
faith healing
telepathy
premonitions
astrology
oracles
witches
superstitions

b Write an imaginative story or poem on a supernatural theme.

c Talk to people about the supernatural and write down any opinions and experiences you find interesting.

d Describe the most frightening sounds you have heard:
   a from a radio
   b from television
   c from the environment during the day
   d from the environment during the night
   Try to say exactly *why* they frightened you.

e Find out as much as you can about some of the following:

Ancient Egyptian religions
African tribal customs
Aztecs and Incas
Spanish Inquisition
Germanic folklore
Oriental folklore

and any others you find interesting.

the interview on a cassette tape-recorder. Most of these have built-in microphones and battery power, so 11-year-olds can easily manage them. The most interesting interviews can be selected and played to the whole class towards the end of the course for information and discussion.

d The reactions here are purely subjective, although it is interesting to discuss why, say, an owl hooting at night can be frightening, whereas during daylight hours it would be only interesting.

e The information for this section may be easily found in many encyclopaedias.

Having discussed the homework tasks, pupils will attempt each section and homework will thus be continued for most of the term. It is worth saying at this stage that after half-term, music with acting (music-theatre), or with dance, or mime, or slide projection, will be possible. The pupils' own stories and poems will be useful then, and if they can paint pictures or make costumes and masks during the first half of the term, such 'extras' can be used in pieces made in the second half of term. (It is often a very useful subject for art departments to exploit, the two approaches to the same subject being mutually beneficial!)

Practical work   The eerie and the unusual in supernatural events provide a natural way of introducing some sound-transformation devices. If three-speed tape-recorders are available, the possibilities for exciting and expressive work are increased dramatically. It is worthwhile spending a lesson showing how (by recording a variety of sounds—owl hoots, humming, a scream, various percussion sounds like one cymbal clash, claves, tambourine, etc.) these sounds can be transformed.

Sounds recorded at the middle speed and then played back slowed down become much more unusual and effective. Even more effect is achieved by recording sounds at the fast speed and then replaying them at the slow speed. (Pupils can easily identify what they are doing by referring to 'fast', 'middle', and 'slow', which respectively indicate a tape-speed of 19, 9.5, and 4.8 cms per second, the normal standard for three-speed tape-recorders.) The opposite procedure—recording sound at the slow speed and replaying at a faster one—is also useful, but often produces a humorous result, rather than an atmospheric and eerie effect.

Reverberation units give an added dimension to sound—one of distance and space—and such effects are most useful, as is the use of an echo chamber. Small devices like these will be in constant use and are well worth the money. Apart from the demand, they contribute to most effective work, and if results are impressive, very positive feedback effectively raises the general expressive potential. Such devices also extend aural perception and sensitivity to sound, encouraging critical listening.

If possible, each group should have a three-speed tape-recorder. The lesson which follows is one of experimentation—recording a variety of sounds at different speeds and listening to the results when replayed. It is

worth pointing out that slowing sound down also makes it last longer, and that length is an important part of any composition. Devices like 'reverb' and 'echo' are invariably over-used at first, but, given time, groups usually manage to control and exploit such devices effectively.

Having acquired some ability in handling this equipment and knowing how to create some effective sounds, the first piece of the course can be attempted. Discussion of this forms the next part of this key lesson. (If no tape-recorders or other devices are available the above lessons can be ignored, as it is quite possible to run this course without such equipment.)

Poems   As there has not been sufficient time for much homework to have been done at this stage, some poems provide an appropriate basis for the initial practical work, giving both content and structure to musical expression. A number of poems can be duplicated for this purpose (see pages 26–27), and these can be used in several ways.

a *Spells*. Such spells as 'A Cure for Blotches' and 'A Cure for a Burn or Scald' can be chanted in a 'witch-like' manner, with atmospheric background sound. A poem like 'The Hag' can suggest various sound effects—horses' hooves, a storm, the wind, etc.—which can be combined with the words to make an effective whole.

b *Music*. Pupils can compose music which effectively mirrors the words and which also adds to the expressive whole, taking its structure from the poem. The poem 'Chant Before Battle' provides a good example, and a piece could be structured as follows:

1 Music to set the scene—before dawn, misty, eerie, a sense of foreboding. This suggests slow-moving, low-pitched sounds, perhaps with an occasional 'owl-hoot'. Vocal glissandos recorded and replayed at a slower speed can be effective here. Towards the end of this section the first verse of the poem could be whispered menacingly.

2 The music gradually changes with the introduction of drums and more aggressive sounds, although remaining fairly quiet. The speed and volume gradually increase as the second verse is chanted, becoming more exciting and fearful.

3 The music takes on the aspect of a battle, and the final verse is almost shouted, the climax of the piece occurring with the last line of the poem, where the 'death-blow' can be most effectively sounded!

Such pieces could be presented as tape-recorded compositions, or could combine some recorded sounds with live instrumental and vocal sounds.

At this time, while discussing the effective use of words and instrumental sounds, it could be useful to play to the whole class the 'Incantation of the Witch of Endor' from Honegger's *King David*. This is an excellent example of how words can effectively be declaimed, and of how music can heighten the effect and content of words.

Some groups may prefer not to use words but instead to develop ideas in sound, exploiting the effects obtained from three-speed tape-recorders and other available devices. Such work could be based on titles like 'An Eerie Moment', or 'Haunted House', etc. If available, a recording of 'An Eerie Moment' from Gunther Schuller's *Seven Studies on Themes of Paul Klee* is well worth playing to the whole class—following discussion of the above starting point. It is an effective example of how changes of speed, volume and texture can be used to convey 'an eerie moment' in a short space of time.

Some groups may well prefer to write their own poem to use for this first piece, and it is likely that much material so produced will be very useful. It is particularly satisfying for groups if they are responsible for both words and music. A typical example of such poetry follows:

Black Witch

The night is dark, the shadows appear,
The black witch is seen, so very near.
In the cottage where she casts spells
Obnoxious vapours fill the air.

Beware, Beware
The black witch is there.
Her black cat stares with illuminated eyes
As her twig-like fingers grasp the wooden ladle,
And as she stirs her evil magic
Her blood-thirsty cackles echo in the room.

Beware, Beware
The black witch is there.
Her shaggy hair covers her face as she shuffles to the door,
Her boney hand clasps the handle of the splintered door,
The rusty hinges give a sudden screech
And the door springs open wide.

Beware, Beware
The black witch is there.

There are thus two possible ways of generating music for the initial piece of the course, and following this Key lesson groups will need at least three weeks to prepare for a performance. With care, performances can be timed to take place in the lesson before the half-term holiday so that a new piece can be started after the break.

Supernatural Poems

Magic Song

(To be recited when in sudden danger)

You earth,
Our great earth!
See, Oh see:
All these heaps
Of bleached bones
And wind-dried skeletons!
They crumble in the air,
The mighty world,
The mighty world's
Air!
Bleached bones,
Wind-dried skeleton,
Crumble in the air!
Hey-hey-hey!

TRADITIONAL: TRANSLATED P. FREUCHEN

Traveller's Curse after Misdirection

May they stumble stage by stage
On an endless pilgrimage,
Dawn and dusk, mile after mile,
At each and every step, a stile;
At each and every step withal
May they catch their feet and fall;
At each and every fall they take
May a bone within them break;
And may the bone that breakes within
Not be, for variation's sake,
Now rib, now thigh, now arm, now shin,
But always, without fail, THE NECK.

R. GRAVES

The Hag

The Hag is astride,
This night for to ride;
The Devill and shee together:
Through thick, and through thin,
Now out, and then in,
Though ne'er so foule be the weather.

A thorn or a Burr
She takes for a Spurre:
With a lash of a bramble she rides now,
Through Brakes and through Bryars,
O're Ditches and Mires,
She follows the Spirit that guides now.

No beast, for his food
Dares now range the wood
But husht in his lair he lies lurking:
While mischiefs, by these,
On land and on Seas,
At noone of the Night are a working.

The storm will arise,
And trouble the skies;
This night, and more for the wonder,
The ghost from the Tomb
Affrighted shall come,
Cal'd out by the clap of the Thunder.

R. HERRICK

A Cure for Blotches

As our blessed Lady sat at her bowery Dower,
With her dear daughter on her knee,
Waiting on the snock snouls and wilfier,
And the Ceronsepel coming in at the town end.
By the name of the Lord I medisen thee.

TRADITIONAL

Chant Before Battle

Let fog fill the skies,
let the cloud cover them,
the winds howl high up
to the world away down,
listen! the wind howls
from far away down!

Shuddering the spear
is charging, is flying,
the twin-bladed shark,
and the footsteps hurtling.
O furious the footsteps,
blood-wet the footsteps
bound for the world's brink.

He goes, god of battles,
the stars in his stride
and the moon in his stride—
run, run from the death-blow!

ANON.: TRANSLATED R. OPPENHEIM
AND A. CURNOW

Charmes

Bring the holy crust of Bread,
Lay it underneath the head;
'Tis a certain Charm to keep
Hags away, while Children sleep.

Let the superstitious wife
Neer the childs heart lay a knife:
Point be up, and Hafte be downe;
(While she gossips in the towne)
This 'mongst other mystick charms
Keeps the sleeping child from harms.

Hang up Hooks, and Sheers to scare
Hence the Hag, that rides the Mare,
Till they be all over wet,
With the mire, and the sweat:
This observ'd, the Manes shall be
Of your horses, all knot-free.

ROBERT HERRICK

Witches' Song

The owl is abroad, the bat, and the toad,
    And so is the cat-a-mountain,
The ant and the mole sit both in a hole,
    And the frog peeps out o' the fountain;
The dogs, they do bay, and the timbrels play,
    The spindle is now a-turning;
The moon it is red, and the stars are fled,
    But all the sky is a-burning:
The ditch is made, and our nalis the spade,
With pictures full, of wax, and of wool;
Their livers I stick, with needles quick;
There lacks but the blood, to make up the flood.
    Quickly DAME, then, bring your part in,
Spur, spur, upon little MARTIN,
Merrily, merrily, make him sail,
A worm in his mouth, and a thorn in's tail,
Fire above and fire below,
With a whip i' your hand, to make him go.
    O, now she's come!
    Let all be dumb.

BEN JOHNSON

A Cure for a Burn or Scald

There came Three Angels out of
    the East;
The one brought fire, the other
    brought frost—
    Out fire; in frost,
In the name of the Father, and
    Son, and Holy Ghost.
Amen

TRADITIONAL

27

KEY LESSON 2 *Music-theatre starting points*

This lesson may be fairly lengthy, as there are many starting points to discuss. These are detailed below:

Music with slides **a**   EAV have produced two very useful programmes combining filmstrips with music, and these can be a very good way of rekindling interest at the resumption of the course. *Night on a Bare Mountain* combines Musorgsky's music with images from Bosch's 'Garden of Delight'. This can act as a useful model for groups who wish to devise their own music and slides. As some art work will (hopefully) have been completed already on the theme, a number of pictures can be made into slides, the music illustrating the slides which could act as a sort of 'narrative', almost telling a story; or the slides could simply add an atmospheric visual focus, enhancing the performance of a piece.

A second, most useful piece from EAV, uses Saint-Saëns's *Danse Macabre*. The visuals used in this piece are of a cartoon type, being made from a series of paintings. Pupils seem to find this presentation particularly effective, possibly because the paintings used in the filmstrip are not particularly sophisticated. The poem on which Saint-Saëns based his music is by Henri Cazalis; it is duplicated on the record sleeve by EAV.

The programmes can form the subject for very interesting discussion about how effective people think the music is: whether the poem has been effectively portrayed in music; whether it could be improved in any way; etc. Classes often request repeat playings of the *Danse Macabre*, and often groups will base their work on this idea. The poem on the facing page, written after the above lesson by a 12-year-old boy shows how stimulating it can prove:

Dance Macabre

A black hole opens,
A hooded, hunch-back horror
Glides out, and, as if by signal,
Weird, ethereal forms dart in the pale blue glow.

Who are they?
Certainly no strangers.
   They are dead,
               dead,
                    dancing dead!

The glow gets greener,
Brighter.
Figures can be seen,
Green faces in the glow.

Sunken mouths
Eyeless sockets
Schools of skeletons
A corps of corpses
All flitting to an unheard rhythm.
They'll dance,
          dance,
              dance macabre!

For eternity
The unearthly threnody continues.
Then the cock crows,
                  twice
And the spectres vanish
      into the growing dawn.

Other useful pieces worth playing include the last two movements of Berlioz's *Symphonie Fantastique*. If such music is used as a stimulus for creative writing, the results can be included as assignment **b** on the homework sheet. With adequate discussion, very sensitive results are possible.

b Slides can be made of ruined buildings, graveyards, churches, etc., so that a variety of possibilities can be presented in this medium. A series depicting sunset, growing evil, midnight, and the climax of activity, dawn, can lead to interesting and successful work.

Music-theatre **a** By this stage of the course many stories and poems will have been written, and these can be used as the basis for pieces in which the story is acted out together with sound-effects and music. If possible, costumes and masks can be made, thus combining several different forms of expression.

b The starting point for such work could be the production of a kind of 'radio play'. This would, of course, be recorded on tape. Having completed this, a group could then devise a mime to give additional expression to the play.

c Many dances can be devised on this theme, and *Danse Macabre* is a useful starting point. Costumes can become very elaborate, and if the music can be recorded on tape, the whole group can be involved with the dance. Alternatively, perhaps some members of the group will play the music live while two or three perform the dance. A description of one such piece was written by one member of a group:

The instruments that we used were drum, guiro, violin, and cymbal. Twelve strikes of midnight start our piece off. We are all lying on the ground. The violin creaks and in turn we get up. Then the drum starts slowly. The witch in our group stays in the middle playing the drum. The guiro then comes in. The violin plays slowly and there are bangs on the cymbal. It gets louder and louder and we go round fast. Then slower until we hear six strikes of dawn. There is one crash on the cymbal and one last creak on the violin. We all slowly lie under our graves.

d Rituals and customs discovered in **Section e** of the homework sheet can also be a useful starting point for music-theatre. Very colourful costumes can be a result of such work, and the subject-matter of these legends can help provide ideas for the musical content and structure, as well as for theatre.

e A separate worksheet can be prepared which makes use of the poem 'The Lyke-Wake Dirge'. This can be made into a piece of music-theatre combining ritual, costume, words, and music. The worksheet is on page 33, and, as suggested, masks and costumes can be an important part of the piece. One girl described her group's working of this poem as follows:

The instruments we use are the gong, cymbal, drums, maracas, castanets, tambourine, chime-bars, wire brush, and beaters. The atmosphere of our piece of music is very eerie and quite slow. At first we have twelve chimes of midnight on the gong. At the sixth gong the cymbal gets higher and higher until it gives a crash on the twelfth chime. Then we use our voices whispering the poem with the tambourine beat. We also have the drum with the beat—we use the wire brush and a beater. The beat is slow. We have the chime-bars on low notes and a few shakes of the maracas. All the time we have the cymbal going quietly. At the end of each verse we have a few shakes of the maracas. At the end everything stops except for a roll on the drums and a shake of the maracas.

This can result in most evocative music-theatre.

f A lengthy and complex piece of music, or music-theatre, or 'radio play' type of piece can be generated from the worksheet based on the witches' scene from *Macbeth*. Because this is a difficult and potentially complex piece, only a few groups may find it useful. The two pages of the worksheet are: (1) the text; (2) suggested working structure; they may be found on pages 34–35. Any group using this worksheet will need quite a lot of help, particularly when planning out their piece.

Results

At the end of this second Key lesson groups can choose their starting point and spend some time discussing how they will develop ideas and realize their pieces. There should be about six weeks for these to be put together, and if performances are scheduled for the last week of term, groups can end their first year in the school with a feeling of real achievement, particularly as many areas of expression are being combined.

Resources

EAV
Night on a Bare Mountain. Danse Macabre.
   Two programmes which combine a record with a filmstrip, *Danse Macabre* in particular being recommended.

Listening material

Berlioz: *Symphonie Fantastique* (movements 4 and 5).
Schuller: 'An Eerie Moment' from *Seven Studies On Themes of Paul Klee*
Honegger: 'Incantation of the Witch of Endor' from *King David*

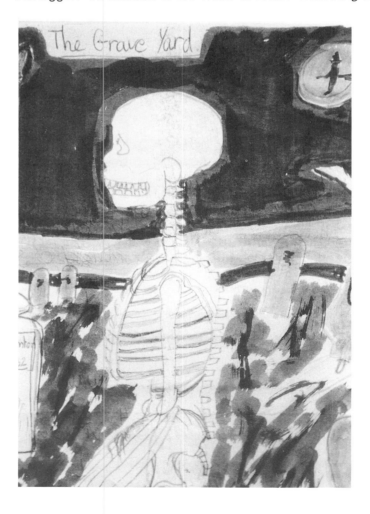

Supernatural
Worksheet for 'A Lyke-Wake Dirge'

These verses come from North Yorkshire where, in the Middle Ages, it was believed that after death the soul travelled over Whinny Moor to Purgatory. They used to be sung at funerals until the 19th century.

A Lyke-Wake Dirge

This ae night, this ae night,
  Every night and all,
Fire, and fleet, and candle-light,
  And Christ receive thy soul.

When thou from hence away art passed,
  Every night and all,
To Whinny-muir thou comest at last,
  And Christ receive thy soul.

From Whinny-muir when thou mayest pass,
  Every night and all,
To Brig o' Dread thou comest at last
  And Christ receive thy soul.

From Brig o' Dread when thou mayest pass,
  Every night and all,
To purgatory fire thou comest at last
  And Christ receive thy soul.

If ever thou gavest meat or drink,
  Every night and all,
The fire shall never make thee shrink
  And Christ receive thy soul.

If meat or drink thou ne'er gavest nane,
  Every night and all,
The fire will burn thee to the bare bane,
  And Christ receive thy soul.

This ae night, this ae night,
  Every night and all,
Fire, and fleet, and candle-light,
  And Christ receive thy soul.

You may care to make this into a ritual describing the journey of the soul. Think carefully about costumes, masks, processions, scene, candles, etc.

Supernatural Worksheet for 'Macbeth'

Witches' scene from 'Macbeth' (*Act 4, Scene 1*)

SCENE A cavern. In the middle a boiling cauldron. Thunder. Enter three witches.

1st witch Thrice the brindled cat hath mew'd.
2nd witch Thrice and once the hedge-pig whined.
3rd witch Harpier cries: 'Tis time, 'tis time.
1st witch Round about the cauldron go;
In the poison'd entrails throw.
Toad, that under cold stone
Days and nights has thirty-one
Sweltered venom sleeping got,
Boil thou first i' the charmed pot.

All Double, double toil and trouble;
Fire burn and cauldron bubble.

2nd witch Fillet of a fenny snake,
In the cauldron boil and bake;
Eye of newt, and toe of frog,
Wool of bat, and tongue of dog,
Adder's fork, and blind-worm's sting,
Lizard's leg, and howlet's wing,
For a charm of powerful trouble,
Like a hell-broth boil and bubble.

All Double, double toil and trouble;
Fire burn and cauldron bubble.

3rd witch Scale of dragon, tooth of wolf,
Witches' mummy, maw and gulf
Of the ravin'd salt-sea shark,
Root of hemlock digg'd i' the dark,
Liver of blaspheming Jew,
Gall of goat, and slips of yew
Sliver'd in the moon's eclipse,
Nose of Turk, and Tartar's lips,
Finger of birth-strangled babe
Ditch-delivered by a drab,
Make a gruel thick and slab:
Add thereto a tiger's chaudron,
For the ingredients of our cauldron.

All   Double, double toil and trouble;
Fire burn and cauldron bubble.

2nd witch   Cool it with a baboon's blood,
Then the charm is firm and good.

ENTER HECTATE

Hectate   O! well done! I commend your pains,
And every one shall share i' the gains.
And now about the cauldron sing,
Like elves and fairies in a ring,
Enchanting all that you put in.

(Eerie music and a song
beginning 'Evil spirits . . .)

2nd witch   By the pricking of my thumbs,
Something wicked this way comes.
Open, locks,
Whoever knocks.

The music should set the scene and atmosphere for the following:

1 A stormy night. A cavern in the side of a hill, eerie and dark, full of flickering shadows. In the middle of the cavern a fire burns beneath a cauldron. Weird shapes can be seen in the shadows—various ingredients for the making of spells and potions hanging from the roof. The whole place reeks of evil . . .

2 An explosion of frightening music.

3 The entrance of the three witches (three motives of sound, one for each witch).

4 Background music for each of the witches' speeches. Use the sound motive for each witch in turn to introduce them (as the spell progresses the cauldron bubbles more fiercely; the music should represent this and also indicate the addition of all the gruesome ingredients to the cauldron).
    The chorus, 'Double, double toil and trouble . . .', should have the same music each time it appears. It could be sung or chanted.

5 Another explosive, frightening outburst of music for the entrance of Hectate.

6 **Write an eerie poem/spell/supernatural incantation.** This begins with the words 'Evil spirits . . .' and the witches sing or chant these words as they move around the cauldron, casting their evil into the boiling liquid. The music at this point must be suitably evil, but should also be rhythmical and repetitive, suggesting the dance-like movements of the witches circling the cauldron.

7 A sudden interruption. The music becomes very still—almost silent.

8 The witches intone their final words.

9 The piece ends with increasingly fearful music describing the 'something wicked' approaching and ending with an enormous explosion of sound.

Seasons
Homework sheet

Spring   Summer   Autumn   Winter

Choose one of the seasons and answer the following questions:

a   Find and describe customs and festivals associated with the season you have chosen.

b   Describe the pattern of your life as influenced by the season: for example, clothes, food, outdoor and indoor activities.

c   Describe your feelings during and about this season.

d   Make a list of at least six words connected with the season. Explain the connection.

e   Make a list of any sounds you associate with the season.

f   Find and copy two poems which to you describe the quality of the season.

g   Make up a story or poem related in some way to the season.

h   Collect pictures, news-items, articles, etc., which have a connection with the season.

Seasons

Aims To develop musical and mixed-media expression from personal and imagined experience.

Equipment Classroom percussion instruments and tape-recorders. Access to art equipment (sugar paper, paints, etc). If possible, 35 mm camera and colour-slide film.

Structure This course is particularly suitable for the first term of the second year. It falls naturally into two sections.

KEY LESSON 1 ## *Seasonal customs*

The first part of this lesson is a discussion of the homework sheet (see page 36), and every pupil should be given a copy. It is worth discussing all the various tasks with the class at this stage. As the weather is a particularly ubiquitous topic of conversation there should be no shortage of contributions from the class. Although all the tasks are self-explanatory, some discussion does give either confidence or reassurance. For example, such customs as Christmas (in its pagan sense), maypole dancing, harvest festival, etc., can be stimulating, and pupils may know of other subjects peculiar to different parts of the country and different cultures (for example, morris dancing, rolling oranges down hills at Easter, customs associated with other religions).

Discussion of the worksheet
This need not be particularly lengthy, but it is worth exploring some ideas from each section. The first piece is based on a poem, either one made up by the group or one provided.

The second part of this first Key lesson thus consists of the distribution and discussion of a number of poems associated with the subject (some examples are given on pages 42–45).

Poems There are two ways of making use of these poems. Either the general mood of the poem can be taken and expressed in sound, the music thus becoming an abstract representation of the season growing out of the poem, or the words of the poem can be set in some way or other. It is easiest, and most effective, if the words are spoken rather than sung, as pupils of this age find

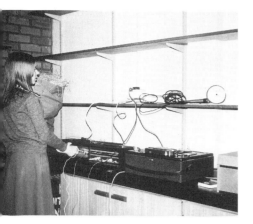

it easier, as a general rule, to create expressive music of an atmospheric kind rather than to be bound by the strict confines of tonality.

A January Night

Hardy's poem 'A January Night' (see page 42) is a good example of a poem which can be successfully set. A discussion of this poem would lead to a suggested way of producing a piece for performance.

The general feeling, or atmosphere, is cold and becomes increasingly eerie. Sounds are suggested in the first verse which can be used throughout the piece to create a suitable background: 'rain', 'wind', 'snarls', 'quivering', 'wheezes'—all suggest various vocal sounds. These could be recorded on tape and played back slowed down to give an eerie effect. Similarly glissandos created on cymbals (a continuous tremolo while the cymbal is alternately lowered into and raised from a tank of water), occasional 'quivers' from maracas, etc., are all quite possible and effective uses of sound. It is possible to make a lengthy tape-loop of such sounds which can then be played continuously with variations made in the playback volume.

The first verse could then be read, almost whispered, over this 'background', thus setting the mood for the whole poem. The second verse would introduce more movement:

The tip of each ivy-shoot
Writhes on its neighbour's face;

These words could perhaps be the signal for some intertwining melodies to be introduced on melody instruments, and the increasing tension of the words

There is some dread afoot

could signal the introduction of drum-beats, soft at first, and maybe various chords and clusters played on piano, organ, melodica, etc., all building towards the climax of the piece in the third verse, around the words

Is it the spirit astray

After this peak the music would gradually calm down and end as it began, with the background atmospheric music gradually fading away. Winter, being the season of death, may suggest the musical character of a death march for some groups.

It is quite possible for groups to make decisions with regard to structure, instrumentation, mood, etc., before starting work on any poem, and it is worth insisting on some sort of plan from each group before they start practical work. If they have a clear idea of what they are trying to do and some idea of how they are going to do it then their work will have direction. At the same time they will still be able to try out ideas as they occur to them in practical work.

Another Winter poem

One group of boys produced an excellent piece on the theme of winter using a poem they made up:

Under a parasol of hissing snow
The grey old lady of winter arrives.
The heart-throb of the forest stills,
And the frozen stream is petrified into immobility.

This poem was read near the beginning of their piece, which was in two sections.

It began with a march-like, slow-moving, two-note ostinato figure played on the low notes of the piano. The poem was read while a slow, sad tune was added, played in the middle register of the piano. The second section introduced a drum which took over the rhythm of the ostinato. Maracas were occasionally shaken. High-pitched, single-note repetitions and some glissandos on the piano completed the sound content of this section,

and the piece gradually faded away, ending with one shake from the maracas.

The group further developed their ideas by producing five chalk drawings of various winter scenes, the first being of a figure representing 'the grey old lady of winter' and the later ones mirroring the words of the poem, representing cold, frosty, winter scenes. These pictures were made into slides and the subsequent combination of slides with music resulted in a most successful expression of one aspect of winter.

During this first Key lesson it is worth discussing the possibility of making slides from pictures and also making costumes for mimes or dance. Such 'extras' can be useful in the second part of the course.

Having discussed a few poems and talked in general terms about each season—winter being the dormant or dead season, spring one of growth and renewal, etc.—each group should be in a position to work at a piece for performance a few weeks later. At the same time as this practical work they will be collecting a variety of information/stimulus material in their homework tasks.

KEY LESSON 2 *Preparing for performance*

There are many possible developments following the performance of the first piece. Any costumes, masks, pictures, and/or slides which have been collected or made during the first part of the term can be used, as can the information which has been researched for homework.

Starting points

a **Music combined with slides** can be most effective, as described above. If pictures have been found or drawn they can be made into ordered sequences, either as pictures to be held up during performance, or, better still, projected as slides. Sequences showing winter landscapes, storms, summer scenes, growth of plants in spring, harvest scenes, etc., can provide a visual stimulus for music and also provide musical structure. (For example, a cold, bleak winter scene; a storm approaches; a blizzard; end of the storm; sun-drenched snow-scene; or a picture of bare earth; leafless trees; shoots appear and push their way through the earth; buds form on branches and turn into leaves; bulbs grow from green shoots into clusters of buds and then into masses of different colours. Such sequences can easily be transformed into ordered sound structures.)

b **Slides** can provide an atmospheric background through which **dance** or **mime** can be performed, the accompanying music being pre-recorded on tape. Some groups may well construct costumes and masks so as to represent the 'gods' of the different seasons, and so small 'suites' may be devised to show the changing seasons.

c **Music-theatre**. Sometimes a member of a group will write a story which can then be used as the basis for a piece of music or for music with acting or mime. One group of girls wrote a poem, produced a piece of music to go with it, and then designed and made suitable costumes for performance. This was called *Oriental Summer*.

The performance of the piece began with the four girls appearing and moving towards their instruments, which were placed on a table in the centre of the stage. Their costumes were kimono-like and they had flowers in their hair. They bowed to the audience in oriental style, and then played a rhythmic introduction on xylophone, then glockenspiel, then cymbal and tambourine. The music then became pentatonic in character. The middle section was without any definite rhythm, consisting of glissandos and tremolos on cymbal and tambourine. During this section the poem was spoken, the different lines being spoken by different people:

> The oriental garden
> Filled with enchanting flowers;
> And the songs of love birds
> Forever beautiful in the sunlight.
>
> An array of flowers
> Flourish in the warmth of the sun;
> And the delicate scent
> And the fragrance of thyme.

The music then returned to the opening material and concluded with a simple pentatonic coda. The girls replaced their instruments on the table, bowed to the audience, and left the stage in what they thought was an oriental manner—very small steps. The ritual and costumes contributed significantly to the performance.

d Less ambitious, but still effective, pieces can take **aspects of the weather** as the title, such as 'Fog', 'Thunderstorm', 'Sunshine', 'Blizzard', etc.; the music can be in the form of effective miniatures.

Just as with many of the other courses described, if the art department can be involved formally in this course, very effective costumes, masks, props, and pictures can be made which will greatly enhance the second piece of the term. Groups would plan their second piece following the second Key lesson, and would probably need most of the second half of the term to prepare it for performance.

Resources

Vivaldi: *The Four Seasons*
Vaughan Williams: *Sinfonia Antartica*
Delius: *North Country Sketches* (particularly Autumn and Winter)
Schuller: 'An Arab Village', from *Seven Studies on Themes of Paul Klee*.
Honegger: *Pastorale d'été* (released by EAV as a record with accompanying filmstrip of summer scenes taken in Switzerland).

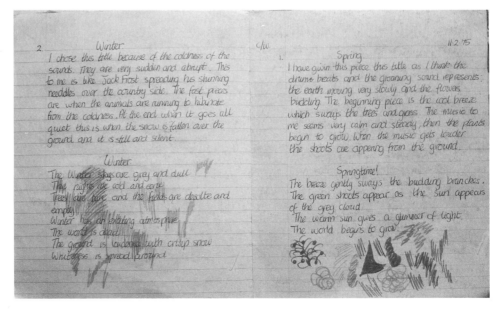

Seasons
Worksheet for poems

Wild Iron

Sea go dark, go dark with wind,
Feet go heavy, heavy with sand,
Thoughts go wild, wild with the sound
Of iron on the old shed swinging, clanging:
Go dark, go heavy, go wild, go round,
    Dark with the wind
    Heavy with the sand,
Wild with the iron that tears at the nail,
And the foundering shriek of the gale.

ALAN CURNOW

October

Certain branches cut
certain leaves fallen
the grapes
         cooked and put up
for winter

mountains without one
shrug of cloud
no feint of blurred
wind-willow leaf-light
their chins up
in blue of the eastern sky
their red cloaks
wrapped tight to the bone

DENISE LEVERTEV

Fog

The fog comes
on little cat feet.
It sits looking
over harbour and city
on silent haunches
and then moves on.

CARL SANDBURG

A January Night

The rain smites more and more,
The east wind snarls and sneezes;
Through the joints of the quivering door
  The water wheezes.

The tip of each ivy-shoot
Writhes on its neighbour's face;
There is some dread afoot
  That we cannot trace.

Is it the spirit astray
Of the man at the house below
Whose coffin they took in today?
  We do not know.

THOMAS HARDY

Thaw

Over the land freckled with snow half-thawed
The speculating rooks at their nests cawed
And saw from elm-tops, delicate as flower of grass,
What we below could not see, Winter pass.

EDWARD THOMAS

Rain

The fitful alterations of the rain,
When the chill wind, languid as with pain
Of its own heavy moisture, here and there
Drives through the gray and beamless atmosphere.

SHELLEY

Snow

In the gloom of whiteness,
In the great silence of snow,
A child was sighing
And bitterly saying: 'Oh,
They have killed a white bird up there on her nest,
The down is fluttering from her breast!'
And still is fell through that dusky brightness
On the child crying for the bird of the snow.

EDWARD THOMAS

Autumn

The falling leaves
    fall and pile up; the rain
        beats on the rain.

GYODAI TRANSLATED BY H. G. HENDERSON

Spring

Nothing is so beautiful as spring—
   When weeds, in wheels, shoot long and lovely and lush;
  Thrush's eggs look little low heavens, and thrush
Through the echoing timber does so rinse and wring
The ear, it strikes like lightnings to hear him sing;
  The glassy peartree leaves and blooms, they brush
  The descending blue; that blue is all in a rush
With richness; the racing lambs too have fair their fling.

GERALD MANLEY HOPKINS

Idyll

In the grey summer garden I shall find you
With day-break and the morning hills behind you.
There will be rain-wet roses; stir of wings;
And down the wood a thrush that wakes and sings.
Not from the past you'll come, but from that deep
Where beauty murmurs to the soul asleep:
And I shall know the sense of life re-born
From dreams into the mystery of morn
Where gloom and brightness meet. And standing there
Till that calm song is done, at last we'll share
The league-spread, quiring symphonies that are
Joy in the world, and peace, and dawn's one star.

SIEGFRIED SASSOON

Summer

A soft Sea washed around the House
A Sea of Summer Air
And rose and fell the magic Planks
That sailed without a care—
For Captain was the Butterfly
For Helmsman was the Bee
And an entire universe
For the delighted crew.

EMILY DICKINSON

Pendulum Poem

Leaves fall
The air is full
Of the fall of leaves.
The spouts in the eaves
Choke with elm,
Ash, oak
And maple shavings.
The yellow rain
Seeps to the drain
Down the white wall,
Whitewash and white
Smooth-cast and plaster.
The last leaves
Leave the tall
Bare sycamore
And lie on the iron
Rails of the square
Where rust is brown
As a young girl's hair.
The leaves lie
Over the eyes,
Moist yellow eyelids
Blear the light,
Blind the skies.

November fires
Burn in gardens,
And Martinmas turns
Oak and ash
To ash and smoke.
The charred leaves
Float in the air;
And soot is sharp
On the dry tongue.
Bright memories
Fall through the mind:
The yellow carpels
Of a flowering youth.
And hand on hand,
Or mouth on mouth,
Find falling leaves
Brittle on fingers,
Dry on the teeth.
In the after-evening
The leaves fall
Slowly as snow,
And bury the night
Under yellow drifts
In the lamp light.

NORMAN NICHOLSON

On a Midsummer Eve

I idly cut a parsley stalk,
And blew therein towards the moon;
I had not thought that ghosts would walk
With shivering footsteps to my tune.

I went, and knelt, and scooped my hand
As if to drink, into the brook,
And a faint figure seemed to stand
Above me, with a bygone look.

I lipped rough rhymes of chance, not choice,
I thought not what my words might be;
There came into my ear a voice
That turned a tenderer verse for me.

THOMAS HARDY

45

Dimensions
Homework sheet

Horoscopes and Astrology

Define the words 'horoscope' and 'astrology'.
Find out the origins of horoscopes and how astrology began.
What is your zodiac sign?
Describe the characteristics of people born under that sign.
Compare your personality with those characteristics.
Interview people and write an account of how horoscopes influence their lives.

Planets and Astronomy

Define the words 'planets' and 'astronomy'.
Find out the names and qualities given to the planets by earlier civilizations.
Write about the solar system; galaxies; black holes; white dwarfs; etc.

Space travel

a Find out as much as you can about modern space research.
b Using one of the following words as a starting point, write a short story or article about space travel:
2001
Apollo
Alien
Time Warp
Lost Planet
Moonscape
Eternity

Movement through time and space

Make a chart showing movement through a selected area during a certain period of time. This can be of anything that changes.

Dimensions

Aims To develop further individual research; to explore some of the spatial possibilities in music; to generate musical ideas from the environment and also from abstract ideas and the imagination.

Equipment Sugar paper, paint, felt tip pens, etc. Tape-recorders. Slide projector(s).

Structure This course lasts for one-and-a-half terms. It is best started after the half-term break in the Autumn so that groups can be working/researching topics from the homework sheet during this half of the term. After the Christmas holiday groups will thus have a fund of information to draw on, and the longest term of the year in which to attempt up to two quite ambitious pieces. The course is in two parts: an introduction during the second half of the first term; and mixed media work in the following term.

KEY LESSON 1 ## *Horoscopes, Planets, and Space travel (Research)*

The first Key lesson deals with the research as detailed on the homework sheet (see page 46).

Research The homework sheet should be distributed and each of the first three sections explained in some detail, as these form the subjects for research in the ensuing weeks of the course. There are two ways of working from this sheet: individuals may choose to produce work from one section only, in which case considerable detail is expected; or they may produce less detailed work on each of the first three sections.

Notes on the homework sheet

Horoscopes and Astrology
This is a very popular section, as a large number of people regularly read their horoscope in the daily newspaper, and many magazines and comics read by second-year pupils contain horoscopes. Many pupils will take great delight in decorating their work with zodiac signs and some may even construct very large signs for display. Real interest can come from comparing the characteristics of the personality with those supposed to belong to the various birth signs. When interviewing people on the subject, it is a good

idea to use a tape-recorder so that the more interesting parts can either be written up later or a tape of the best comments assembled. This section thus encourages some historical research and also an investigation of present-day attitudes; many pupils will produce beautifully illustrated 'chapters' of work.

Planets and Astronomy

This is another very popular area of study with many pupils. The scope of work to be done has deliberately been left open and again is a combination of the historical and the factual. Many school
textbooks (and the Physics department) have a considerable amount of information on the factual aspects, and the school library is bound to have several encyclopedias in which the historical information can be found. Often a few pupils will have books on the subject at home, and occasionally a keen amateur astronomer will have his own telescope and will obviously contribute much to discussion on this area of the worksheet.

Space travel

This section is in two parts:

a *Modern space research*. Such questions as 'What is going on?' 'What has been accomplished?' 'What is going to happen in the next few years?' will stimulate the class. Again it is likely that some pupils will be quite knowledgeable on the subject, and, as with 'Planets and Astronomy', the school should have a considerable amount of information on the subject.

b The list of words are a few suggestions for imaginative writing. Invariably many more suggestions will come from the class. It is possible for pupils to produce quite good ideas — short science fiction type stories — using one of these words (or one of their own) as a title. Some will no doubt read science fiction magazines, and many of the pictures in such publications are very colourful and evocative.

Having explained how these three sections can be worked, pupils should be in a position to pursue their chosen area(s) for homework during the first half term or more of the course. This information will be used in practical work during the second part of the course, which allows pieces to be produced using the above three areas as starting points.

Movement through Time and Space

For the first half term of the course practical work is developed from this fourth area on the sheet. Practical work can begin almost immediately, and there are three possible starting points.

Practical work **a** The instructions on the worksheet can be developed into a **musical score**. If, for example, the number of cars, lorries, buses, cyclists, pedestrians, etc., passing the school gates (or any suitable location) is noted in 30-second blocks of time over a period of about ten minutes, this information can then be converted into instructions for a piece of music. If only a few vehicles pass during the first ten minutes then the timing begins again and more events recorded until sufficient information has been collected. The results of this — an activity which pupils seem to enjoy — could look like the chart opposite.

Notes on the chart

The chart can be converted into a musical score, using large sugar paper. For this particular chart, six instruments would be needed. Lorries could become drums, buses a piano, cars an organ and so on. Just as in the PATTERNS course each instrument can be represented by a different shape and colour. The number recorded for each 30-second block of time can have

	0'00"	0'30"	1'00"	1'30"	2'00"	2'30"	3'00"	3'30"	4'00"	4'30"	5'00"	5'30"	6'00"	6'30"	7'00"	7'30"	8'00"	8'30"	9'00"	9'30"	10'00"
Lorries				1			3			1		1		2			2			1	
Buses			3			1			2						1		1				
Cars		2			1		3	4		2	3		1		3	4		2	4		
Motor bikes				1							1					1					
Cycles		2				1	2		1			1	1				2				
People			3		1	2	7			5		1		3	1			3	2	4	

many different meanings, and the group has to decide on the most effective interpretation. (The number could mean how many times a sound is made; how loud or soft it is; how high; how low; etc.) Quite large and colourful scores can be produced which will take two or three weeks to rehearse. Each 30-second block on the original chart should be reduced to about 15 or 20 seconds on the score, thus resulting in a piece approximately three minutes long.

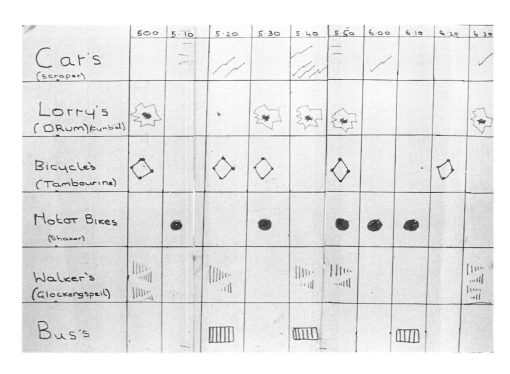

Other starting points which can be worked in this way include, for example, the number of hours of sunlight or inches of rain recorded in various cities over a period of time, or the number of goals scored by various football clubs in a certain number of matches; any set of numbers can be useful in this context.

b A second possible starting point is the production of a **musical mobile**. This is again a further development of the ideas explored in the PATTERNS course in the first year. In this course a moving score can be constructed and played.

Groups by this stage will be very familiar with the representation of sound as shape and colour. The simplest way to use this kind of representation is to make a series of cards about 12 inches square, possibly of different coloured card. Having made or obtained six or eight pieces of card, the pupils can draw or paint different symbols on each side of the cards in a variety of colours, such symbols representing the different sounds which may be made using instruments.

A frame made by joining wire coat-hangers together is easily constructed, and the finished cards can then be suspended from the frame with different lengths of cotton. If the whole mobile is suspended from the ceiling in some part of the room and the group assembles round it with a variety of instruments a fairly random but nevertheless enjoyable piece can be performed. The mobile should move quite gently, thus presenting an ever-changing set of instructions for performance. It is worthwhile including some blank surfaces on the mobile to represent silence! Too much sound can be messy and often one of the 'rules' for performance which develops is that each symbol should be played only once when it appears.

Balloons can be covered with papier mâché and symbols subsequently added, or small boxes can similarly be used. Thus several different shapes could be used to make the mobile and it would be possible to confine, say,

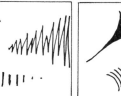

drums to instructions which are on the oval shapes, melody instruments to those on boxes, and other instruments to square (triangular, round, etc.) pieces of card. There are many possibilities which can be explored with this assignment.

The third possible starting point is one which focuses on **spatial effects**. A piece called 'echoes' implies two groups which can be widely separated, one group perhaps visible to an audience, the other hidden. The instrumentation of the two groups is important here. If they are identical, should the material they play be the same but with a difference in volume? Is it possible to echo pitched sounds using only non-pitched instruments? Such questions can quickly generate many musical ideas.

Another way of using the idea of echoes is to construct a long tape-loop and run this between two tape-recorders. One recorder would be in record mode, the other in playback mode. A microphone should be placed so as to pick up the live sounds made by the group. These are then recorded on the first tape-recorder. A few seconds later this material will be heard replayed by the second tape-recorder. Interesting and sometimes complex canons can thus be created, and with care the microphone can pick up not only live sounds from the group but also the repetitions from the second tape-recorder to give very complex and impressive textures.

Among the several poems which can be exploited spatially are 'Pendulum Poem' by N. Nicholson and '40–Love' by Roger McGough.
'*Pendulum Poem*' (see page 45 in the SEASONS course).
This poem suggests the left to right motion of a swinging pendulum, and if two people were narrating this poem they could be placed to the left and right of an instrumental group. Each line of the poem naturally falls into two parts—left and right—so that the words are always moving across the space. The instrumental players could be placed in the centre, or similarly grouped to the left and right to emphasize the spatial element.

'40—Love'
This is reproduced on page 64. In this version the words themselves have been spatially separated and some rhythmically entertaining pieces can be generated quite readily from this material.

Having explained and discussed these three possible starting points—the chart or graph, the mobile, the use of spatial effects, and the poems—groups will make their decision and spend some time collecting information, making a mobile, perhaps writing a poem. Some lessons will then be needed for rehearsal time, so that this first part of the course should easily last for six or seven weeks; if it is begun in the second half of a term, the holiday will provide a suitable break before the more ambitious, mixed-media pieces are attempted.

Drawing together

This lesson draws on the information which should have been gathered in the course of the first half term's homework. Each of the first three sections can generate many ideas for musical or mixed-media pieces.

Horoscopes and Astrology

There are two fairly obvious ways of producing work from this section:

a The star sign of each member of the group can be used as the basis for the piece, the characteristics of the sign being translated into sound (thoughtful, gentle, aggressive, cold, etc.). Some groups may additionally make costumes which use the star signs and prepare mimes or dances to give expression in movement as well as sound. Other groups may take just one star sign and develop a more ambitious piece which concentrates on one 'type' of person or set of characteristics; this can often lead to very effective dances. As with most starting points it is quite possible to produce 'pure' music, or music in combination with other forms of expression, and each group will naturally decide which is the best form for themselves.

An account of a piece based on 'Horoscopes', written by a group of girls, reveals how this subject can act as a stimulus for composition:

Our piece starts with Ruth and Julie playing up the piano, starting slowly on the low notes and getting faster as we go up. At the same time I play the maracas—52 beats—representing the 52 weeks of the year.

I say my horoscope which is Cancer. Cancer can be a pleasant person, so we start off gently at the top of the piano; but Cancer is also very jealous so we bang on the low notes.

Next is Sagittarius. As this is half man, half horse, we do a man walking. This is done slowly on the piano. Then it gets faster until it is a horse galloping. It then slows down to a man walking.

Debbie then says 'Libra'. As this is the scales I play scales on the piano and suddenly go wrong. The slightest mistake makes a Libra person go mad, so we bang on the bottom notes. But among the midst of madness come the scales, that is me playing up the piano. In the end the scales balance up and everything is quiet.

b The signs of the zodiac can be drawn on paper, as can the star pattern as it appears in the sky. This can be used as the basis for a design which will in turn become the score for a piece of music—a useful way of seeing music as well as hearing it. Additionally, a group may take the representation of the zodiac sign (e.g. a fish for Pisces), draw a picture/design reflecting the mood they associate with this, and base their music on this aspect of the star sign. (Although some groups may already have used this starting point in the 'Constellations' section of PATTERNS, they sometimes choose to rework their ideas. As they are older and have more experience of this kind of work they often surprise themselves with their increased ability!)

Planets and Astronomy

There are many ways of firing the imagination and generating music in this section. Work produced tends to fall into one of three categories: descriptive or evocative music; music with slides; music-theatre.

Descriptive music.

The information discovered from homework on the characteristics given to the planets as gods—Mars being war-like, Venus peaceful, etc.—can be exploited in musical terms. Holst's suite *The Planets* is perhaps the best known example of music produced in this way, and these starting points seem to be very stimulating, generating many ideas for music.

Alternatively, the known characteristics of various planets can be exploited in musical terms. Mercury could thus be represented with violent and very

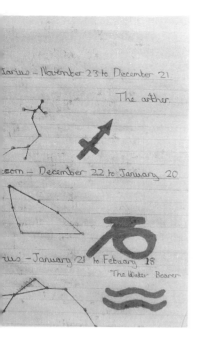

exciting, primitive, music mirroring the intense heat and volcanic activity of that planet. By contrast the moon, being totally barren and lifeless, would call for a very different type of music.

Discussion of such ideas can be very stimulating, particularly as it will involve the sharing of information discovered by individual pupils as part of their homework assignments. By encouraging such interchange of information and ideas considerable enthusiasm can be engendered.

Music with slides

As a result of the increasing interest in space exploration over the past few years many slides of solar eclipses, stars, and galaxies, as well as the planets of the solar system, are readily available. (The school's physics department is probably the closest source!) A sequence of slides showing a rocket launch, a journey through space, a lunar landing, exploration on the surface of the moon, the return from the moon to the earth, and either a safe return to earth or a disaster resulting in becoming lost in the depths of space, gives a clear sequence of events which can suggest an equally clear musical structure and content, giving scope for the expression of many emotions.

Slides of galaxies, nebula, stars, etc., can be very stimulating, as well as contributing to atmospheric performances. Such combinations of slides with music tend to be very effective and to generate a lot of positive feedback, which is very important for future work. Groups working with a slide sequence need space to work, in which the slides can be to hand for projection. This does focus the attention and encourage a large degree of involvement.

Music-theatre

The personification of the planets as gods is easily discovered in the homework section of the course, and a glance at any record cover of Holst's *Planets* suite will give a very usable set of characteristics! Costumes and masks are very useful for this stage of the course, and if these can be made by individuals or groups very effective dances and mimes can be combined with music. Two gods with opposing characteristics can form the basis of a piece as these give the necessary contrast for successful work. More ambitious groups may well attempt to make music-theatre descriptions of several of the gods/planets, ending up by producing fairly lengthy suites.

Space travel

Very ambitious mixed-media pieces can result from this section, as well as descriptive or evocative pieces of music. Any imaginative writing which has been done for homework can be used, either as a direct part of the piece (music with words), or to give some help with structure, content, mood, etc. Use of electronic effects—reverberation, phasing, echo, etc.—can contribute significantly to this work, and pieces with titles such as 'Alien', 'Moonscape', 'Lost Planet', and so on, all lead the imagination forwards—there is rarely any lack of musical ideas. Similarly any stories or poems which have been written can become the basis for 'radio plays' combining speech, sound-effects, and music.

As in the 'Planets and Astronomy' section, many slides can be used, either as sequences involving effective atmospheric music, or as background projection through which music-theatre, dances or mimes can be performed.

At the end of this second Key lesson, groups will have a large number of possibilities from which to choose. It is worth spending some time in discussion at this point. Each group should carefully plan its piece at this stage, asking such questions as 'What is the subject?' 'What instruments will be needed?' 'Are any electronic effects/tape-recorders needed?' 'Would slides feature in the piece?' ('If so, which slides are needed?') 'Will any costumes be needed for any dance, mime, or acting? ('If so, can they be borrowed from drama, or made at home or in needlework lessons?') Will scenery, masks, etc., be useful?' ('If so, can these be made in art lessons?').

Any time spent considering such points is time well spent, and if such 'extras' as costumes, props, etc., can be made in other lessons while work continues on the musical aspects, a complete piece will gradually evolve, and considerable momentum and enthusiasm be generated.

The work planned by groups at this stage could well take a complete term to prepare, depending on the complexity and scope of the piece. Some groups will no doubt choose pieces which are less ambitious than this and so be able to work two shorter pieces—one in each half of the term. So many possibilities can be generated by this course that interest can easily be sustained for this length of time, and it is likely that groups will produce the most effective (and lengthy) pieces they have so far constructed. Final performances may well have to be spread over two weeks.

Occasionally there will be a particularly talented group capable of complex mixed-media work even in their second year. An extended piece, suitable for such a group, is given on an extra worksheet (see pages 55–56). Suggested ways of developing ideas, based on a short story, are given on the sheet. Because of its potential complexity I suggest this only as a possible starting point to groups who are prepared to put in a lot of work extra to curriculum time.

Listening

There is considerable scope for listening during this course, but rarely as a class activity. It is better to direct groups to specific pieces which are particularly relevant to them at the appropriate time on the course. For example, if a group had made a piece on 'space mystery' or 'eternity' then they might find 'Neptune' from *The Planets* of interest; 'Mars', from the same work, would be an obvious piece for a group to listen to if they had worked on a piece 'Mars: God of War'.

Groups will listen carefully and critically if they are involved with the subject. Often they will listen at some length and this is, of course, a very welcome result from working in this way.

Resources

EAV have produced an excellent series of filmstrips under the title 'Exploring the Universe'. Pictures of lunar exploration, imaginative drawings of future space stations, space craft, planets. Photographs of galaxies, star clusters, nebulae, etc., are to be found in these film strips.

Several sets of slides are available from the Science Museum in London which include many pictures taken by various space probes and also of lunar exploration.

Other listening material

Holst: *The Planets*
R. Strauss: *Also Sprach Zarathustra* (opening sequence)
Sibelius: *Pelléas et Mélisande* ('At the castle-gate' is the music used in the television series 'The Sky at Night')
Music from the film *2001* (and other sci-fi films)
Tangerine Dream: *Rubicon, Alpha Centauri, Hyperborea*
Subotnick: *Silver Apples of the Moon*

Dimensions
Worksheet for extended mixed-media piece

The following story has been divided into two main parts. The first section is concerned with a problem and its effects, and the second section with the solution. The climax of the story comes at the end.

Use tape-recorders and devise a production which uses music to make the story more atmospheric, exciting, interesting and meaningful. The final tape could well sound like a radio play. Be very careful that the words of the story are clear and not unintentionally drowned by the music.

When the tape is completed you may also—if you wish—devise a mime to be performed with the tape. This could include the use of costumes and of pieces of art work made into slides for projection during the mime; you may also include a short section (about four minutes) of movie film.

Sole solution

Part one

He brooded in the darkness and there was no one else. Not a voice, not a whisper. Not the touch of a hand. Not the warmth of another heart.

Darkness.

Solitude.

Eternal confinement where all was black and silent and nothing stirred. Imprisonment without prior condemnation. Punishment without sin. The unbearable that had to be borne unless some mode of escape could be devised.

No hope of rescue from elsewhere. No sorrow or sympathy or pity in another soul, another mind. No doors to be opened, no locks to be turned, no bars to be sawn apart. Only the thick, deep sable night in which to fumble and find nothing.

Circle a hand to the right and there is naught. Sweep an arm to the left and discover emptiness utter and complete. Walk forward through the darkness like a blind man lost in a vast, forgotten hall and there is no floor, no echo of footsteps, nothing to bar one's path.

He could sense one thing only and that was self.

Therefore the only available resources with which to overcome his predicament were those secreted within himself. He must be the instrument of his own salvation.

How?

No problem is beyond solution. By that thesis science lives. Without it, science dies. He was the ultimate scientist. As such, he could not refuse this challenge to his capabilities.

His torments were those of boredom, loneliness, mental and physical sterility. They were not to be endured. The easiest escape is via the imagination. One hangs in a strait-jacket and flees the corporeal trap by adventuring in a dream-land of one's own.

But dreams are not enough. They are unreal and all too brief. The freedom to be gained must be genuine and of long duration. That meant he must make a stern reality of dreams, a reality so contrived that it would persist for all time. It must be self-perpetuating. Nothing less would make escape complete.

So he sat in the great dark and battled the problem. There was no clock, no calendar to mark the length of thought. There were no external data upon which to compute. There was nothing, nothing except the workings within his agile mind.

And this one thesis: no problem is without solution.

Part two

He found it eventually. It meant escape from everlasting night. It would provide experience, companionship, adventure, mental exercise, entertainment, warmth, love, the sound of voices, the touch of hands.

The plan was anything but rudimentary. On the contrary it was complicated enough to defy untangling for endless aeons. It had to be like that to have permanence. The unwanted alternative was swift return to silence and the bitter dark.

It took a deal of working out. A million and one aspects had to be considered along with all their diverse effects upon each other. And when that was done he had to cope with the next million.

And so on . . . on . . . on . . .

He created a mighty dream of his own, a place of infinite complexity schemed in every detail to the last dot and comma. Within this he would live anew. But not as himself. He was going to dissipate his person into numberless parts, a great multitude of variegated shapes and forms each of which would have to battle its own peculiar environment.

And he would toughen the struggle to the limit of endurance by unthinking himself, handicapping his parts with appalling ignorance and forcing them to learn afresh.

He would seed emnity between them by dictating the rules of the game. Those who observed the rules would be called good. Those who did not would be called bad. Thus there would be endless delaying conflicts within the one great conflict.

When all was ready and prepared he intended to disrupt and become no longer one, but an enormous concourse of entities. Then his parts must fight back to unity and himself.

But first he must make reality of the dream. That was the test!

The time was now. The experiment must begin.

Leaning forward, he gazed into the dark and said, 'Let there be light.'

And there was light.

E. F. RUSSEL

People

Aims To encourage objective musical expression growing from observations of other people and the more common emotions of everyday experience. Also to encourage objective questioning and communication.

Equipment Standard classroom instruments. Tape-recorders, particularly portable cassette-recorders.

Structure This course is particularly suited to the first or second term of the third year. It is in three main sections.

KEY LESSON 1 *People: social problems*

Discussion of the worksheet

The content of this lesson is a discussion of the first page of the worksheet (page 59), the homework part of the course. All pupils have access to printed material from newspapers, magazines, comics, etc., and often enjoy collecting pictures and articles and subsequently presenting them in booklet form. As much variety as possible should be encouraged, articles and pictures about people from all walks of life being useful. Although this section occupies little space on the worksheet it can be the most time-consuming part, and result in a considerable amount of work.

The second section of the worksheet gives ideas for interviewing people who may be part of some pupil's everyday life. It is worth spending some time on 'Questions you may care to include' with regard to *how* such questions can be put. A sympathetic, interested attitude on the part of the interviewer will yield the best results! Often pupils may care to tackle this part of the course in groups of two or three. It is also possible to make use of portable cassette-recorders for this activity and either submit an edited version of the cassette, or copy out the more interesting parts of interviews. Some pupils may get to interview only one or two people, but others often manage several. Often a greater sympathy and sensitivity towards others is developed, and it can be worthwhile to spend a lesson later in the term listening to and discussing the results of various interviews.

Practical work A very short initial exercise for practical work in the following lesson is a 'piece' using only **voices**, these being the primary means of communication

between people in day-to-day life. Different accents are interesting to discuss and attention can be directed towards inflection and quality rather than to words themselves. The *way* people talk is very important. (For example, it is possible to say 'Oh! Stop it.' and mean two completely different things. The instruction 'Sit down and be quiet' can be given in the style of a sergeant major, or of a very timid person unsure of themselves. Each will have a different effect which can be identified and discussed.)

By using only vocal inflection, no real words, it is quite possible to convey many attitudes or emotions: sternness, snootiness, rudeness, silliness, poise, anger, affection, uncouthness, etc. As an initial exercise groups can prepare, either on tape or for live performance, a short vocal piece illustrating one or several differences but using inflection to do so. This should take only one lesson to prepare, with performances being given in the second lesson. Much objective discussion/criticism should naturally accompany these performances.

KEY LESSON 2   # *People and their emotions*

Discussion of the worksheet

The second page of the worksheet forms the discussion area of this lesson (page 60). There is a certain amount of written work required for this which can be done either in class time or at home (although they have homework from page 1 of the worksheet), and this work can be done on an individual or a group basis.

Some discussion of each of the four emotions is useful:

'What causes you to be angry/depressed?'

'What does it feel like physically/mentally?'

'What do other people look like when they are happy/fed up?'

Practical work

The practical work which follows this lesson makes use of all available **sound sources**, not just voices. The task is to create a piece called either 'Anger', 'Peace', 'Depression', or 'Joy', or any other emotion. A clear idea of instrumentation and structure should be thought out by each group before practical work is begun.

At this point the difference between self-expression and expression in a more objective sense may become clear. Somebody who is angry or frustrated may bang things around—so a group may take a number of drums and cymbals and make a tremendous noise. This may release some of their tension but would leave most listeners rather bored. Anger tends to come in waves, beginning with a build-up of tension, followed by partial release, further build-up, release, etc., until the final moment of release or destruction. A useful example is 'Mars' from Holst's suite *The Planets*, although it is slightly long. A shorter, but very effective example of a short outburst in musical terms is 'An Eerie Moment' from Schuller's *Seven Studies on Themes of Paul Klee*. The point to stress is that groups should be as objective as possible and should try to convey their chosen emotion in musical terms. The distinction should be drawn between others experiencing something as a result of successful communication, and the performing group experiencing their emotion with instruments in their hands while the listeners merely observe them so doing! Some very clear thinking and planning is called for on everybody's part.

The preparation of this piece, using instruments with or without voices, should take a few weeks and the performance lesson could be timed to coincide with half-term. The second half of the term could thus begin with another key lesson.

People
Worksheet 1

a   Collect articles and pictures from newspapers and magazines on individual people, groups of people, and social problems.

b   Where possible interview a person or number of people from the list below. Write an account of this interview, or tape-record the interview and add your own comments later.

a   an elderly person
b   a blind person
c   a deaf person
d   a person with some other handicap
e   a schoolteacher
f   a dustman
g   a shop assistant
h   someone with their own business
i   someone unemployed
j   a housewife
k   a policeman
l   a gypsy
m   a lorry driver
n   a farm worker
o   a factory worker
p   someone who lives alone
q   a foreigner
r   someone in entertainment

Questions you may care to include in your interview:

'What makes your life different from that of people not in your situation?'

'What are the main problems in your way of life?'

'What advantages are there in your way of life?'

'What do you think of older people?'

'What do you think of younger people?'

'What would you most like to change in your way of life?'

'What changes would you like to see in society generally?'

'How do you spend your leisure time?'

'Is there much difference between what you do in your lesisure time and what you do at work?'

'Which do you most enjoy—work or leisure?'

'If you were completely free to choose, with enough money, time, good health . . . what would you do?'

People Worksheet 2

Anger

frustration	loud
conflict	jagged
hatred	harsh
violence	explosive

Peace

harmony	smooth
calm	probably slow
love	probably quiet
completeness	gently curved

Depression

sadness	deep
melancholy	dark
loneliness	heavy

Joy

exuberance	brilliant
enthusiasm	glowing
vitality	moving
vividness	exciting

a   Describe at least one of these emotions in your own words. Add to the words above when describing the emotion.

b   Write in detail about a real or imagined incident which involves you personally in one of the above emotions.

c   Find and copy a poem to illustrate your chosen emotion, and then make up a poem of your own on an emotion.

d   Write down how you think an emotion can be represented in sound, pictures, movement, shape, colour, etc.

KEY LESSON 3 *Blind people*

By this time groups should have interviewed several people listed on the first page of the worksheet and should also have collected many articles and pictures. They should therefore have quite a store of useful information. An excellent way of beginning this stage of the course is to give each person an insight into the world of the blind. To do this the whole class needs to leave the classroom and initially assemble at one end of the longest corridor in the school. (Staircases are best avoided!) The task is to walk from one end of the corridor to the other without looking, and although there might be some giggles at first, after each person has taken more than a few steps its more serious aspects become apparent. As sound becomes very important, it is worthwhile encouraging as much quietness as possible. A second very useful area in which to do this activity is somewhere out of doors. Walking from one side of the playground to the other 'blind' can be very illuminating, so to speak, and the uneven surfaces of playing fields are also very useful. Outside, the feel of wind, sunlight, the smells in the air, the surrounding sounds, all become much more vivid when 'blind', and these experiences form a very useful area of discussion when back in the classroom.

From this a discussion of some of the interviews is a natural progression, particularly if any blind people have been interviewed. The deaf and physically handicapped can similarly be discussed, as can other people who have been interviewed, and any suitable tapes of interviews can usefully be played to the whole class at this time.

Poems

Section **c** of the worksheet may have resulted in some good poetry being found or written which can similarly be introduced to the class, and this is also an excellent moment to introduce a separate poem sheet (see pages 63–64 for some examples).

Practical work

From all this the practical work will develop. The task is to take the characteristics of one person, or several, either from the interviews or from pictures, and to produce a musical expression of these. Some very useful examples of how this has been done in the past can be played and discussed.

a 'The Gnome' from Musorgsky's *Pictures from an Exhibition* is a useful musical portrait, and 'Samuel Goldenberg and Schmuyle' from the same work is an excellent extension of the first work attempted on the course, the vocal piece. In Musorgsky's movement the inflection is given with instruments. Samuel Goldenberg, the rich, ostentatious, and domineering person being represented by heavy unison strings and woodwind, while the poor Schmuyle, whining and snivelling, is represented by a muted trumpet.

b A more transparent, evocative description of a person can be found in 'La fille aux cheveux de lin', No. 8 of the first book of Debussy's piano preludes. Elgar's *Enigma Variations* contain a wealth of musical description and representation of differing physical and mental characteristics, and a lesson spent considering some of these can be very fruitful.

c Some groups may care to take one of the poems and set this instead of the above assignment. One group produced some effective work using 'Ozymandias' as their text.

Their piece began with a depiction of a desolate desert landscape using cymbals and glissandos produced by scraping a wire brush across the lower strings of a piano. A violin or cello bow drawn across the edge of a cymbal produces very interesting sounds, and these two basic sounds were present as 'background' throughout the piece. Next, a plaintive melody was played on recorder, in the distance.

Following this, slow drum-beats, very soft at first but gradually becoming louder, were introduced to coincide with the opening narration of the poem. The music gradually increased in volume and speed, with some snatches of the recorder melody occasionally played, until the climax of the piece, where a new voice declaimed,

My name is Ozymandias, king of kings:
Look on my works ye Mighty, and despair!

This was spoken with some reverberation, and the opening recorder melody was played very loudly in octaves on the piano.

The piece ended with a return to the opening music, and the final three lines of the poem were read with suitable expression. The recorder, this time played with a considerable amount of reverberation, played part of the melody and the cymbal ended the piece.

d   The e. e. cummings poem on the poem sheet (page 63) gives scope for further extension of the ideas exploited in the initial vocal piece of the course.

Pictures

As with other courses, visual stimuli can play an important part, and many pieces of music can take pictures (either drawn by pupils or collected from magazines) as their starting point. An example of such a piece can be heard in the tape/slide programme *Music at Notley*. A picture of someone's grandmother formed the starting point for this piece, which tells of the woman sitting by the fire and daydreaming of her past life. It uses glockenspiel, cymbal, and piano, and the different memories of the grandmother form the different sections of the piece, all of which are combined into a successful whole.

Work on such pieces can last for the whole of the second half of the term, performances providing a satisfactory conclusion to the course.

If such performances are given and there are one or two lessons still left, an excellent way of concluding the course is to suggest that each group produces a musical portrait of someone in the school. The final lesson of the course then contains several pieces which describe people in the class or various members of staff—always a winner!

Resources

Debussy: *Préludes* for piano, Book I
Elgar: *Enigma Variations*
Holst: *The Planets*
Musorgsky: *Pictures from an Exhibition*
Schuller: *Seven Studies on Themes of Paul Klee*

People
Poems

The Cowherd

The grass spreads across the common for six or seven miles;
In the evening breeze he plays on his pipe three or four notes.
Home again for a plenteous meal after the yellow dusk,
Without doffing his grass-coat he sleeps beneath the moon's radiance.

LU YEN

Brother

It's odd enough to be alive with others,
But odder still to have sisters and brothers:
To make one of a characteristic litter—
The sisters puzzled and vexed, the brothers vexed and bitter
That this one wears, though flattened by abuse,
The family nose for individual use.

ROBERT GRAVES

Two Clocks

There was a clock in Grandad's house:
black, gold-numbered,
and a three-foot pendulum.
I'd hear it tick out endless Christmases,
fingering patches on the green velvet

Such splendour. His chair.
His knife. His fork. 'Wait!'
Grandma would say,
'till your father gets in!'
Twisting my mother to a girl again.

Revenge needs time. 'That junk,'
my mother said,
and burned the clock,
the velvet, the Blessed Are the Pure in Heart
in red and gold behind the bed.

And brought him back to live with us,
where bleak electric hands swirled gently,
slicing her days and his
into thin fragments.

JOHN DANIEL

Girls in a Factory

Seated in rows at the machines
Their heads are bent; the tacking needle
Stitches along the hours, along the seams.

What thoughts follow the needle
Over the fields of cloth,
Stitching into the seams
Perhaps a scarlet thread of love,
A daisy-chain of dreams?

DENIS GLOVER

ygUDuh

          ydoan
          yunnuhstan

          ydoan o
          yunnuhstan dem
          yguduh ged

          yunnuhstan dem doidee
          yguduh ged riduh
          ydoan o nudn
LISN bud LISN

            dem
            gud
            am

            lidl yelluh bas
            tuds weer goin

     duhSIVILEYzum

                e e cummings

63

Ozymandias

I met a traveller from an antique land
Who said: two vast and trunkless legs of stone
Stand in the desert . . . Near them, on the sand,
Half sunk, a shattered visage lies, whose frown,
And wrinkled lip, and sneer of cold command,
Tell that its sculptor well those passions read
Which yet survive, stamped on these lifeless things,
The hand that mocked them, and the heart that fed:
And on the pedestal these words appear:
'My name is Ozymandias, king of kings:
Look on my works, ye Mighty, and despair!'
Nothing beside remains. Round the decay
Of that colossal wreck, boundless and bare
The lone and level sands stretch far away.

SHELLEY

The Fortune-teller

By the ancient rill there is a single plum-tree
That refuses to be imprisoned in garden or park.
Far away in the mountain depth it fears not the cold
As though at hide-and-seek with Spring.
My inmost thoughts, who can know them?
Ties of friendship are hard to make.
Alone in my romance, alone in my fragrance,
The moon comes to look for me.

CHU TUN-

As foolish as monkeys till twenty or more;
As bold as lions till forty and four;
As cunning as foxes till three score and ten;
Then they become asses or something—not men.

TRADITIONAL

40
middle
couple
ten
when
game
and
go
the
will
be
tween

love
aged
playing
nis
the
ends
they
home
net
still
be-
them

ROGER MCGOUGH

Communication

Aims To explore mixed-media forms of expression taking the starting
points/stimulus from 'extra-musical' sources which are of particular concern
or relevance to pupils of this age.

Equipment All the equipment which has been used in the previous years should be
available for use.

Structure This course is an ideal way of ending the curriculum music course in the
third year. All the available equipment can be exploited, end results tend to
be powerful, and it serves as a useful summing up of the lower school music
course.

It naturally falls into two parts, a short introductory exercise followed by a
more lengthy and complex piece.

KEY LESSON 1 ## *T.V. Advertisements*

At this stage there is no printed information to distribute, this lesson
consisting of listening and discussion. A tape needs to be made before the
lesson consisting of a number of varied television advertisements. As much
variety of style as possible should be represented—different types of music,
techniques, appeals—and this is then played to the class for critical listening,
analysis, and discussion.

Starting points 'How is the product being sold?'
'On its own merits, or because using/possessing it will lead to greater
happiness/more friends/women/money/a better job . . .?'
'What section of the population is it aimed at—children, housewives, working
mothers, teenagers, sportsmen . . .?'
'How does this affect the content/form of the advert?'
'What qualities in the soundtrack/music make it effective?'
'Is it successful?'

There are many fruitful areas for discussion and it is also very interesting
to observe the initial reaction to the soundtracks of advertisements alone.
The removal of the visual element seems to encourage close listening, many
pupils being quite surprised when they listen closely and critically to material
they have only half-heard (often many times) previously.

Practical work

Following this comes the first practical assignment of the course. Each group is given the task of **producing their own advertisement**, either as a soundtrack only, or as a combination of sound and some acting. This task should be limited to perhaps one or two weeks' work and as many sound-effect units as possible should be available. Reverberation, fuzz-boxes, filters, echo-chambers, etc., are all most appropriate for this assignment, as are three-speed tape-recorders.

The results from this initial piece of work are invariably entertaining, some being closely modelled on a particular advert, some being quite sarcastic, some being a serious and original effort. The important point is involvement with communication. The more serious part of the course is in the second part of the term.

When these first pieces are performed it is worth discussing how visuals could improve the overall effectiveness of the presentation, or if some acting was part of the piece, how this contributed to the result. This then leads to the second section of the course.

Nuclear weapons, smoking, and pollution

These three areas for investigation are all fairly wide-ranging. Consequently it is normally possible to pursue only one with any single class, although if several third-year classes are following the course then each can pursue a different topic. The three areas are **nuclear weapons**, with some emphasis being placed on Hiroshima, **smoking**, and **pollution**. One of these forms the subject of the following Key lesson or lessons, so each will be dealt with separately.

KEY LESSON 1 *Nuclear weapons*

Starting points

It would seem that this subject is never going to disappear, and will probably grow in importance during coming years. There is abundant material available for use. I began the Key lesson by showing a film of the bombing of Hiroshima. This was available from county stock in the 20th-century history section. It showed the background to the raid and included film shot at the time of the incident—both of the dropping of the bomb and of its after-effects.

Clearly discussion will follow this, and the soundtrack of the film can usefully be included here, with special attention being paid to the build-up of tension to lead to the moment of destruction, followed by the devastation and horror resulting from the explosion. Penderecki's *Threnody to the Victims of Hiroshima* is an obvious choice of listening material at this time.

A follow up to this lesson is further discussion of the effects of nuclear war. Many articles are readily available from newspapers, magazines, CND, etc., and these can be very useful ways of provoking intense discussion. (See the example on page 68.) Peter Watkins's film 'The War Game', although dated, is still powerful; the BBC produced a more up-to-date report of the effects of a nuclear explosion above London in a QED programme in 1982.

Poetry is also a very useful source of stimulation, and Peter Appleton's 'The Responsibility' and Peter Porter's 'Your Attention Please' (both page 69) are two very usable examples.

Further listening at this time can include parts of Britten's *War Requiem*, Schoenberg's *Survivor from Warsaw*, Shostakovich's 7th and 8th Symphonies, Martinů's *Memorial to Lidiče*, etc. Relevant extracts from such works can become very powerful in the context of the course.

Practical work   The result of these Key lessons should be a high degree of motivation to give expression to the thoughts and feelings aroused by the material. Such expression needs to be controlled and structured to be effective, and considerable thought needs to be given by each group before practical work is begun. Extra musical elements, particularly the use of slides—either made by pupils or provided in school—can be very powerful in combination with music/soundtracks. Some suggested structures for practical work are listed below:

a   **A piece combining soundtrack/sound effects/music** to depict the Hiroshima bombing. This could be in three sections:
1   Prelude—full of foreboding and gradually increasing in tension.
2   The raid—the flight of the aircraft, the approach to the city, the release of the bomb, the explosion.
3   The end—destruction, the agony of the survivors, the hopelessness, radiation sickness, death . . .
     Many effective and sometimes moving pieces have resulted from such a basic structure.

b   **A documentary type of programme** which combines factual information with emotive soundtrack/music rather in the style of a radio programme (but slides can, of course, still be most appropriate for this).

c   **An abstract piece** depicting some aspect of the subject. Penderecki's *Threnody* is particularly useful here.

d   **The setting of a poem**, either one written by a pupil or one of those made available. Such pieces may combine words, music, and slide projection to result in very effective expression.

Having made a decision concerning the nature of their work, groups may well take until the end of term to complete their piece. The final lesson—performances—often contains some of the best pieces produced by groups during their three years.

When the living will envy the dead

from Joyce Egginton in New York

THE devastation caused by a nuclear attack would be so intense that life for the few survivors would be 'socially unrecognisable', threatened by famine, disease and genetic damage.

This was the view of leading American scientists and doctors who presented a bleak picture of the consequences of nuclear war to a conference in New York last week.

Dr H. Jack Geiger, professor of community medicine at New York's City College, painted a nightmare picture of what would happen if New York was blasted by two powerful nuclear bombs.

A nuclear bomb followed by a second within a few hours would leave 14 million dead 'and would so disrupt the social fabric that the word survival would be meaningless,' Dr Geiger said.

Most hospitals would be destroyed. Most doctors and nurses would be dead. Those remaining, even if they were willing to risk further radiation, would be unable to get to victims through the fires and debris which would engulf the city.

A conservative calculation is that each surviving and functioning physician will have 1,700 injured to care for. Most victims will die without even drugs to ease unbearable pain, and the living will envy the dead.'

Dr Geiger predicted mass firestorms which would turn fall-out shelters into crematoria. Severe injuries from burns would be superimposed upon radiation effects, and lethal amounts of fall-out would spread for hundreds of miles. Millions more deaths from infections and radiation-induced disease would follow.

The lack of water, sanitation and uncontaminated food would soon take as many lives as direct injury.

Yet there would be no way to dispose of the millions of decomposing corpses — which would not only add to the likelihood of epidemics but cause 'profound emotion disorders' among the survivors.

'Given these effects, I believe that any physician who even participates in so-called civil defence planning is committing an unethical act,' he said. 'To do so is to imply to the public that a coherent and effective medical response is possible — and that implication would be a lie.'

He said he was not trying to frighten, but to inform. 'The idea that there can be limited nuclear war does not make sense in any biological, human, political or realistic terms.'

Dedicated

The conference was called by a new movement dedicated to revealing the medical and social consequences of a nuclear war. Many movement members worked on the development of nuclear fission.

Another kind of nuclear attack was envisaged by Professor Bernard T. Feld of the Massachusetts Institute of Technology who worked on the first nuclear chain reaction. He said a scenario being discussed by American military strategists involved an exchange of atomic bombs between the United States and the Soviet Union, each trying to eliminate the other's nuclear arsenals.

If atomic bombs were to be rained on missile storage sites in both countries, Dr Feld predicted that lethal fall-out would cover both nations 'and the onslaught worldwide would be so great that it is questionable whether the human gene pool could withstand it.'

Asked about the chances of a nuclear war by the end of the century, Dr Feld replied: 'Fifty-fifty, given the kind of stockpiling that is going on. We still have to learn to live in a world in which nuclear weapons are easy to produce, and in which the material to produce them is a by-product of a widely used power source. I can only hope that if a nuclear war starts that there will be such a widespread reaction of horror that it would be brought to an immediate close.'

Professor George Kistiakowsky, of Harvard University, who leads the movement, said the most likely possibility was the use of nuclear weapons by a small nation 'less educated' in the consequences than we are.'

There is an annual average of six local wars, and it seemed quite likely that the super-Powers might be drawn into one of them.

'If there is no public opposition to our own hard-liners and militarists, the probability of our nuclear involvement is almost inevitable,' he said.

Another likely outcome of a nuclear war, according to Professor Henry Kendall of the Massachusetts Institute of Technology, was the displacement of the world's ozone layer followed by global climate alteration.

As well as causing wide-spread forest fires, the unmasked ultra-violet rays of the sun would be so intense that 'for years one would not be able to go outdoors, except swathed and goggled.'

Insects survive

Lacking this protection, many species of animals and plants would die — while insects, which are most resistant to radiation, would proliferate to spread disease throughout a starving world.

'The problems of recovery before the remaining stocks of food and fuel ran out would be a race against time, and it would probably be lost,' Dr Kendall predicted.

'The struggle to allocate the remaining assets among the few million survivors would go on continually until there were only scattered bands of people living at the level of the Middle Ages, but without the social structure that made the Middle Ages work,' he said.

Your Attention Please

The Polar DEW has just warned that
A nuclear rocket strike of
At least one thousand megatons
Has been launched by the enemy
Directly at our major cities.
This announcement will take
Two and a quarter minutes to make,
You therefore have a further
Eight and a quarter minutes
To comply with the shelter
Requirements published in the Civil
Defence Code—section Atomic Attack.
A specially shortened Mass
Will be broadcast at the end
Of this announcement—
Protestant and Jewish services
Will begin simultaneously—
Select your wavelength immediately
According to instructions
In the Defence Code. Do not
Take well-loved pets (including birds)
Into your shelter—they will consume
Fresh air. Leave the old and bed-
ridden, you can do nothing for them.
Remember to press the sealing
Switch when everyone is in
The shelter. Set the radiation
Aerial, turn on the geiger barometer.
Turn off your Television now.
Turn off your radio immediately
The Services end. At the same time
Secure explosion plugs in the ears
Of each member of your family. Take
Down your plasma flasks. Give your children
The pills marked one and two
In the C.D. green container, then put
Them to bed. Do not break
The inside airlock seals until
The radiation All Clear shows
(Watch for the cuckoo in your
perspex panel), or your District
Touring Doctor rings your bell.
If before this, your air becomes
Exhausted or if any of your family
Is critically injured, administer
The capsules marked 'Valley Forge'
(Red pocket in No. 1 Survival Kit)
For painless death. (Catholics
Will have been instructed by their priests
What to do in this eventuality.)
This announcement is ending. Our President

Has already given orders for
Massive retaliation—it will be
Decisive. Some of us may die.
Remember, statistically
It is not likely to be you.
All flags are flying fully dressed
On Government buildings—the sun is shining.
Death is the least we have to fear.
We are all in the hands of God,
Whatever happens happens by His Will.
Now go quickly to your shelters.

PETER PORTER

The Responsibility

I am the man who gives the word.
If it should come, to use the Bomb.

I am the man who spreads the word
From him to them if it should come

I am the man who gets the word
From him who spreads the word from him.

I am the man who drops the Bomb
If ordered by the one who's heard
From him who merely spreads the word
The first one gives if it should come.

I am the man who loads the Bomb
That he must drop should orders come
From him who gets the word passed on
By one who waits to hear from *him*.

I am the man who makes the Bomb
That he must load for him to drop
If told by one who gets the word
From one who passes it from *him*.

I am the man who fills the till.
Who pays the tax, who foots the bill
That guarantees the Bomb he makes
For him to load for him to drop
If orders come from one who gets
The word passed on to him by one
Who waits to hear it from the man
Who gives the word to use the Bomb.

I am the man behind it all;
I am the one responsible.

PETER APPLETON

KEY LESSON 2 *Smoking*

This is a very appropriate subject as virtually everyone is affected by this habit, either as a smoker, or because someone close to them smokes, or because they experience some of the less pleasant results of smoking.

A variety of Key lessons are available by way of introduction:

a A general discussion of smoking, supported by information and posters. The results of regular smoking are of great importance, and descriptions of chronic bronchitis, emphysema, and cancer in a graphic manner, illustrated by slides if possible, can arouse powerful feelings—and also result in several ashen faces! Further areas of discussion centre on money: how the vested interests of the tobacco industry and the Chancellor of the Exchequer seem to be more important than people's health. Such suggestions can lead to very heated discussions.

b A number of films are available which can usefully be shown. It is likely that the central stock of county films will include some useful items (usually available free of charge); the biology department, the Health Education Council, ASH and BBC and ITV can all be useful sources for filmed material. Stimulating discussion invariably follows the viewing of such material.

c It may be possible to arrange for a doctor or nurse to visit and talk to classes. This was done one year at Notley, where a doctor came and gave an excellent talk complete with real lungs for examination and a variety of slides of patients suffering from smoking-induced ailments.

The success of the Key lesson(s) depends mainly on powerful presentation. Because of the nature of the subject matter involvement should present no problem; the more the individual feels the importance of the subject the better, as this leads to greater expressive potential.

Practical work Visual elements can be very powerful in this course and many posters produced by pupils appeared around the school. These can of course be used as part of the practical work, and examples of some schemes are given below:

a **A straightforward anti-smoking advertisement** suitable (say) for a radio broadcast. This can be expanded to become a documentary type of programme including factual information, interviews with a variety of people, and ending with the advertisement.

b **A short play** describing someone acquiring the habit (possibly at school), growing dependence, development of disease, death. One group of girls pursued such a scheme and made a series of slides to illustrate it. These began with adverts showing healthy smiling men smoking cigarettes and progressed via disgustingly full ashtrays and smoke-filled rooms to pictures of illness; the sequence ended with various graveyard scenes. The soundtrack used no words but gave real expression, beginning with pop-type advertising, gradually changing to coughing, wheezing, etc., and ending with a kind of funeral march.

c The most ambitious scheme is **the production of a film**. Although this is far from straightforward, some groups are able to cope with the difficulties. One film produced as part of this course ran as follows:

The opening shot was of the back of a chair set against a gold-coloured, dimly lit background. A back view of the head and shoulders of the chair's occupant are visible, and he is smoking a cigarette. The air gradually becomes full of smoke. The music throughout the film is very subdued, disappearing completely from the moment the echo-chamber is used. From the beginning of the film up to this moment the music consisted of low-pitched chords and clusters played on an organ and piano, toegther with slow drum-beats. These sounds were slowed down by using a three-speed tape-recorder. The film, after a few seconds of the opening shot, changed to a

view of an ashtray full of cigarette ends, matches, etc. A voice is heard calling in the distance,
   'Albert! Albert! Its time for tea!'
The film revealed a smoke-filled atmosphere. The voice, more impatiently this time, calls again,
   'Albert! Albert!'
A different, lower-pitched voice spoke,
   'Albert is dead'
The echo chamber was switched on at the word 'dead', and at the same moment the film revealed the front view of the chair—empty.

This film was a very restrained, economical piece of work which took a great deal of effort, planning, and organization to complete; it was a considerable achievement.

d Less ambitious, **more abstract pieces** were also produced. These concentrated more on some of the sounds which can be associated with smoking: striking matches, clearing the throat, coughing, etc. When recorded and given various treatments—distortion, echo, reverb, ring modulation, speed-changing—some fairly effective results can be obtained, although they do not always make 'pleasant' listening!

Such starting points contain sufficient potential to occupy a group for several weeks, and it is relatively easy for all groups in a class to produce worthwhile work on some aspect of the topic.

Smoking—Britain's king-size tragedy

Philip Jordan on the latest effort to make a nation kick the habit

THE Government should ban all tobacco advertising and immediately introduce a tax system to put cigarettes up to £1 for 20 while putting an ounce of pipe tobacco down to 20p, a leading chest consultant said yesterday.

Dr Leslie Capel of the London Chest Hospital says that it is the only way to persuade the nation to cut down on smoking and so prevent 95 per cent of lung cancer, the most prevalent cancer known to man.

Dr Capel's comments came yesterday after a preview showing of a This Week investigation into smoking and cancer, Dying For A Fag? which will be screened tonight. Dr Capel appears in the programme and warns: "Cigarette smoking is not certain death, but it is probable death. There are people who are going to die miserably because no one has been able to convince them that cigarette smoking causes lung cancer and other diseases. For them, cigarettes have death written on them."

Dr Capel says that large executive cigars and pipes are known to be safer than small cigars and far safer than cigarettes. Ideally, doctors would like to see the Government (which spends £500,000 a year on anti-smoking propaganda while the tobacco industry spends £70 millions pushing the idea) ban smoking altogether.

But, says Dr Capel, "there are old people who will never be able to give up and it would be unfair to them. In addition, the Government is never able to move faster than public opinion, and at the moment public opinion would never stand for the ban. If you ban things, people automatically want to do them."

In the Thames programme, which is the first of a two-part look at the subject, a 42-year-old man, described only as Peter, tells how he was given three years to live after smoking 35 cigarettes a day. He and his German-born wife, Angela, are filmed at their Costa Brava appartment, where they are living his final days.

He says: "I didn't realise it could affect someone so young. I made up my mind to give it up on my fortieth birthday. It lasted about seven hours. At the office the next morning I just reached for the cigarette packet again."

The film reveals that 50,000 people in Britain now die from smoking each year, six times more than die in road accidents. And smoking, particularly among the young and especially among girls, is on the increase. The figures illustrate the failure of a comprehensive report produced by the Royal College of Physicians in 1971 (and Dr Capel was on the panel) to get the message across.

The much-lauded report, Smoking and Health Now, showed conclusively that the number of deaths linked to smoking was increasing rapidly. And showed, too, that among doctors, who had realised what the evidence meant and had stopped smoking, there were fewer cases of lung cancer.

Thames commissioned a Gallup poll to go with the programme which reveals that although 40 per cent of the over-16 population smoke, and 65 per cent of these think that smoking can damage their health, 30 per cent do not believe that cigarettes can kill them, and 13 per cent don't know.

When asked which caused more deaths in Britain now, road accidents or smoking, only 16 per cent of smokers were right. Of the others 63 per cent were wrong and 21 per cent did not know. Of the smokers, 53 per cent said they would approve a ban on cigarette advertising but only 28 per cent would approve increased taxation and only 19 per cent approved a total ban on sales.

There was also little success in trying to give up smoking. Sixty-five per cent of smokers have tried to give up, Gallup showed, but 60 per cent did not think they ever would and of those who thought they would 17 per cent did not know when, and 16 per cent said simply "at some later date."

Dr Capel says that giving up is a desperate, four-stage process: realising the damage smoking can do; realising the damage it can do to one's own health; wanting to give up; and deciding to do so.

"The last is the hardest of all," says Dr Capel. 'Nicotine is a powerfully addictive drug, known to be chemically similar to those that pass messages of pleasure to our brains. Taking it, we cannot help but ask for more." Dr Capel himself says he once smoked an ounce of pipe tobacco and 10 cigarettes a day but gave it up "after my wife complained of the stink."

But, he adds, "when I was a teenager, I know I couldn't go into a cafe to meet my friends without a cigarette hanging from my mouth. It was a symbol of acceptance and it is this image that we have got to change."

The IBA was shown the This Week film before it goes out in case a warning had to be issued about offensive material—particularly scenes of cancered lungs being fished from metal buckets in a hospital laboratory. But the IBA passed it without comment, and Dr Capel says: "Behind those buckets is a volume of tears."

KEY LESSON 3 *Pollution*

Starting points

Yet another aspect of 20th-century living which is causing increasingly serious problems is pollution. Industrial pollution is perhaps the most obvious, but noise pollution, exhaust gases, the destruction of the environment for new towns or fossil fuels, the climatic consequences of destroying rain forests, the destruction of the ozone layer in the upper atmosphere, the death of plant and animal life in ponds and lakes because of acid rain—all these aspects of pollution (and there are many others) can form a most stimulating set of starting points for discussion in an initial Key lesson.

If possible, the Key lesson should include a film illustrating one or more of the above aspects of the subject. There is a variety of sources, including BBC and ITV, the geography and history departments in the school, county sources, and the Shell film catalogue. Newspaper articles, pictures, slides, and poems can similarly be exploited as stimulus material.

Practical work

There are many ways of generating pieces from these starting points, but I have selected four different approaches:

a **A ternary form piece** contrasting the unspoiled tranquillity and beauty of nature with the concrete jungle. The first section of this piece would obviously use gentle sounds, harmonious and perhaps lyrical music. The beautiful effects which can be produced using an echo-chamber are useful here. Some of the sounds of nature, bird-song in particular, can also be imitated musically to good effect in this section.

The second part of the piece can begin suddenly, in complete contrast, or gradually grow out of the first section, taking over and destroying the tone of the opening section. In this section harsh, ugly, discordant, loud music is an obvious way of depicting the destruction and alteration of the environment. A distortion unit ('fuzz-box') is a useful and cheap electronic device which is most appropriate here.

If the ending of the second section is the climax of the piece, being the loudest, most destructive part, the return to the opening ideas can be most effective. The use of reverberation in this section can contribute much to an expression of wistful reflection.

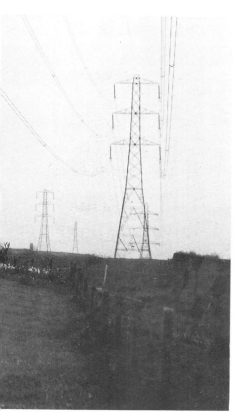

As with other projects, **poems** can provide very useful starting points, as well as suggesting structure and content for musical expression. Of the poems selected (see pages 75–79), Betjeman's 'Parliament Hill Fields' provides a most suitable contrast. Its beginning, mirroring the rhythm of the mechanical train with its polluting sulphur fumes and rumbling, thundering sounds, suggests a variety of textures, rhythms, and sound sources. Honegger's *Pacific 231* is an excellent example of a musical description of a train journey. The contrast found in the final stanza of the poem could result in a two-part musical structure, the first being vigorous, mechanical, ugly; the second more placid and lyrical. A useful parallel here is the last movement of Honegger's *Liturgical Symphony* (Symphony No. 3) which contrasts a violent, destructive march with a vision of peace and tranquillity.

'The Pylons' (page 75) can form the basis of an abstract piece of music, possibly featuring the use of drones and osinato figures representing the flow of electricity across the landscape blighted by the 'quick perspective of the future'. The poem could also be narrated with music, and pictures or slides of pylons could be a useful addition. 'Cleator Moor' (page 77) is another poem which could be treated in this way.

The other poems could similarly act as a stimulus for musical expression, or serve as a text to be set to music. There is an obvious opportunity to encourage pupils' own poetry or prose writing, which can then be used in similar ways.

Pictures, like poems, can also act as a powerful stimulus. 'Children's Playground' and 'River Scene' are both typical of many urban environments.

Children's playground

A discussion of such pictures can often lead to the production of very powerful music.

c   This starting point, like **d**, demands an excursion into the environment. The task is to construct **a documentary type of programme** on some aspect of pollution—or a general survey of the locality. Part of this assignment would consist of interviewing a variety of people, recording the interviews on cassette tape for later use when assembling the programme, and perhaps recording some environmental sounds to include in the programme. The result may be a fairly lengthy tape.

It is important to decide upon the scope of the programme in advance—if there is a local controversy (a new road; an extension to an airport; a new factory; etc.) this can be made use of, but in virtually all environments there is some aspect of pollution at hand. If interviews are conducted, a questionnaire as in the PEOPLE project should be prepared in advance so that relevant information is collected.

When assembling the programme there will be many opportunities for producing 'incidental' music to link the various items. The introductory music could be a piece in its own right, and it could well include pieces ('The Pylons', for example) which a variety of groups have produced on the course, thus combining 'pure' music with documentary. It is possible for a whole class to work at different aspects of this theme, and for a presentation to be devised which combines all such work. Taking slides of the locations investigated or which are relevant to the pieces produced is a further way of extending the expressive possibilities in performance.

d   The fourth piece is specifically **a tape/slide piece**—a kind of environmental collage and commentary.

The first stage is to visit a variety of locations, recording sounds and taking slides. Appropriate places include building sites, railway and bus stations, motorways, shopping centres, airports, factories, etc.

The second stage in the process is to assemble a tape collage of the recorded sounds, devising an order which seems effective. Contrasts are, of course, particularly useful here, and it is quite possible to treat effectively the recorded sounds as in the 'Machines' piece in the PATTERNS project (see pages 18–19).

Having assembled the tape an effective sequence of slides should be selected from those taken. When combined with the tape, very effective pieces can result. An example of a tape/slide piece, the music contrasting harshness with tranquillity, the slides contrasting the countryside with

River scene

factories and pollution, can be seen at the end of *Music in a Creative Education*, a video programme which contains examples of many pieces described in these courses.

Other music which, although not specifically connected with pollution, can be stimulating, revealing how the aggressive and harsh can be effectively contrasted with more peaceful music, includes:

Shostakovich. 5th, 7th, and 8th Symphonies (first movements)
Stravinsky: *Rite of Spring*
Vaughan Williams: 4th Symphony

Conclusion

Communication is ideally suited to the final term—or possibly the last term and a half—of the third year. Pupils have often chosen not to continue with music as a curriculum subject by the middle of their third year, this being the time when many schools operate their 'option' systems and subjects for study in the fourth and fifth years are chosen. This can lead to some pupils becoming unmotivated. Because the subject matter of COMMUNICATION is such as will involve everyone to some degree, and because finished pieces of work can be quite powerful, it is possible to keep virtually all pupils motivated and involved up to the end of term. The results of this course can be the best work produced by groups during their first three years of curriculum music of this sort and can provide an ideal composing basis for further development in GCSE. Listening and performing are also implicit and integral in this style of work.

Resources

Useful addresses

CND: 11 Goodwin Street, London N4 3HQ
Health Education Council: 78 New Oxford Street, London WC1A 1AH
ASH: 5–11 Mortimer Street, London W1
WATCH: 22 The Green, Nettleham, Lincoln LN2 2NR

The video programme (*VHS format*) *Music in a Creative Education*, by Phil Ellis, illustrates many of the pieces described in *Out of Bounds*; it is available from the Midland Centre for Music in Schools, FETT, Birmingham Polytechnic, Westbourne Road, Edgbaston, Birmingham B15 3TN.

Listening

Penderecki: *Threnody to the Victims of Hiroshima*
Britten: *War Requiem*
Schoenberg: *A Survivor from Warsaw*
Martinů: *Memorial to Lidiče*
Shostakovich: *5th, 7th, and 8th Symphonies*
Stravinsky: *The Rite of Spring*
Vaughan Williams: 4th Symphony
Honegger: *Pacific 231*
Honegger: 3rd Symphony

Pollution Poems

The Pylons

The secret of these hills was stone, and cottages
Of that stone made,
And crumbling roads
That turned on sudden hidden villages.

Now over these small hills they have built the concrete
That trails black wire:
Pylons, those pillars
Bare like nude, giant girls that have no secret.

The valley with its guilt and evening look
And the green chestnut
Of customary root,
Are mocked dry like the parched bed of a brook.

But far above and far as sight endures
Like whips of anger
With lightning's danger
There runs the quick perspective of the future.

This dwarfs our emerald country by its trek
So tall with prophecy:
Dreaming of cities
Where often clouds shall lean their swan-white neck.

STEPHEN SPENDER

Parliament Hill Fields

Rumbling under blackened girders, Midland, bound for Cricklewood,
Puffed its sulphur to the sunset where the Land of Laundries stood.
Rumble under, thunder over, train and tram alternate go,
Shake the floor and smudge the ledger, Charrington, Sells, Dale and Co.,
Nuts and nuggets in the window, trucks along the lines below.

When the Bon Marche was shuttered, when the feet were hot and tired,
Outside Charrington's we waited, by the 'STOP HERE IF REQUIRED',
Launched abroad the shopping basket, sat precipitately down,
Rocked past Zwangier the Baker's, and the terrace blackish brown,
And the Anglo, Anglo-Norman Parish Church of Kentish Town.

Till the tram went over thirty, sighting terminus again,
Past municipal lawn tennis and the bobble-hanging plane;
Soft the light suburban evening caught our ashlar-speckled spire,
Eighteen-sixty Early English, as the mighty elms retire,
Either side of Brookfield Mansions flashing fine French-window fire.

Oh, the after tram ride quiet, when we heard a mile beyond,
Silver music from the bandstand, barking dogs by Highgate pond;
Up the hill where stucco houses in Virginia creeper drown;
And my childish wave of pity, seeing children carrying down
Sheaves of drooping dandelions to the courts of Kentish Town.

JOHN BETJEMAN

Cleator Moor

From one shaft at Cleator Moor
They mined for coal and iron ore.
This harvest below ground could show
Black and red currants on one tree.

In furnaces they burnt the coal,
The ore was smelted into steel,
And railway lines from end to end
Corseted the bulging land.

Pylons sprouted on the fells,
Stakes were driven in like nails,
And the ploughed fields of Devonshire
Were sliced with the steel of Cleator Moor,

The land waxed fat and greedy too,
It would not share the fruits it grew,
And coal and ore, as sloe and plum,
Lay black and red for jamming time.

The pylons rusted on the fells,
The gutters leaked beside the walls,
And women searched the ebb-tide tracks
For knobs of coal or broken sticks.

But now the pits are wick with men,
Digging like dogs dig for a bone:
For food and life we dig the earth—
In Cleator Moor they dig for death.

Every waggon of cold coal
Is fire to drive a turbine wheel;
Every knickle of soft ore
A bullet in a soldier's ear.

The miner at the rockface stands,
With his segged and bleeding hands
Heaps on his head the fiery coal,
And feels the iron in his soul.

NORMAN NICHOLSON

Slough

Come, friendly bombs, and fall on Slough
It isn't fit for humans now,
There isn't grass to graze a cow
   Swarm over, Death!

Come, bombs, and blow to smithereens
Those air-conditioned, bright canteens,
Tinned fruit, tinned meat, tinned milk, tinned beans
   Tinned minds, tinned breath

Mess up the mess they call a town—
A house for ninety-seven down
And once a week a half a crown
   For twenty years,

And get that man with double chin
Who'll always cheat and always win,
Who washes his repulsive skin
   In women's tears.

And smash his desk of polished oak
And smash his hands so used to stroke
And stop his boring dirty joke
   And make him yell.

But spare the bald young clerks who add
The profits of the stinking cad;
It's not their fault that they are mad,
They've tasted Hell.

It's not their fault they do not know
The birdsong from the radio,
It's not their fault they often go
   To Maidenhead.

And talk of sport and makes of cars
In various bogus Tudor bars
And daren't look up and see the stars
   But belch instead.

In labour-saving homes, with care
Their wives frizz out peroxide hair
And dry it in synthetic air
   And paint their nails.

Come, friendly bombs, and fall on Slough
To get it ready for the plough.
The cabbages are coming now:
   The earth exhales.

JOHN BETJEMAN

Prayer Before Birth

I am not yet born; O hear me.
Let not the bloodsucking bat or the rat or the stoat or the
   clubfooted ghoul come near me.

I am not yet born; console me.
I fear that the human race may with tall walls wall me,
   with strong drugs dope me, with wise lies lure me,
      on black racks rack me, in blood-baths roll me.

I am not yet born; provide me
With water to dandle me, grass to grow for me, trees to talk
   to me, sky to sing to me, birds and a white light
      In the back of my mind to guide me.

I am not yet born; forgive me
For the sins that in me the world shall commit, my words
   when they speak me, my thoughts when they think me,
      my treason engendered by traitors beyond me,
         my life when they murder by means of my
            hands, my death when they live me.

I am not yet born; rehearse me
In the parts I must play and the cues I must take when
   old men lecture me, bureaucrats hector me, mountains
      frown at me, lovers laugh at me, the white
         waves call me to folly and the desert calls
            me to doom and the beggar refuses
               my gift and my children curse me.

I am not yet born; O fill me
With strength against those who would freeze my
   humanity, would dragoon me into a lethal automaton,
      would make me a cog in a machine, a thing with
         one face, a thing, and against all those
            who would dissipate my entirety, would
               blow me like thistledown hither and
                  thither or hither and thither
                    like water held in the
                      hands would spill me.
Let them not make me a stone and let them not spill me.
Otherwise kill me.

LOUIS MACNEICE

No place

I was brought down
in suburbs;
nurtured on asphalt,
stared up at the sky
through saw-tooth Tudor.
Gates with rising suns,
gardens with plaster dwarfs
bounded by—what?
childhood? I peeped
through featherboard fences
at lawns lost in trees,
tennis courts and space

I knew I could fill.
Now I can go, be
anyone, anywhere, slough
off the concrete shell
of rebellion. Leave my—what?
Self? Like the tennis ball
in somebody's dahlias
tip-toeing quietly away,
afraid of the sudden shout,
and half-hoping it comes.

JOHN DANIEL

Acknowledgements

We are grateful to the following for permission to reproduce their material:

Jonathan Cape Ltd.: '40–Love' by Roger McGough from *After the Merrymaking* (UK and British Commonwealth).

Allen Curnow: 'Chant before Battle' Maori text translated by Roger Oppenheim and Allen Curnow from *The Penguin Book of New Zealand Verse* (1960).

Doubleday & Co. Inc.: 'Autumn' by Gyodai from *An Introduction to Haiku* translated by Harold G. Henderson. Copyright © 1958 by Harold G. Henderson. Reprinted by permission of Doubleday and Co. Inc.

Faber & Faber Ltd.: 'Prayer before Birth' by Louis MacNeice from *The Collected Poems of Louis MacNeice*. 'Cleator Moor' by Norman Nicholson from *Five Rivers*. 'Pendulum Poem' by Norman Nicholson from *Rock Face*. 'The Pylons' by Stephen Spender from *Collected Poems 1928–1985* (UK and British Commonwealth).

Grafton Books (A division of the Collins Publishing Group): 'ygUDuh' by e e cummings from *The Complete Poems 1913–1962* (UK and British Commonwealth excluding Canada).

Harcourt Brace Jovanovich Inc.: 'ygUDuh' by e e cummings from *The Complete Poems 1913–1962* (World excluding UK and British Commonwealth).

Harvard University Press: 'Summer' by Emily Dickinson. Reprinted by permission of the publishers and the Trustees of Amherst College from *The Poems of Emily Dickinson*, edited by Thomas H. Johnson, Cambridge, Mass.: The Belknap Press of Harvard University Press, copyright 1951, © 1955, 1979, 1983 by the President and Fellows of Harvard College.

John Murray (Publishers) Ltd.: 'Parliament Fields' and 'Slough' by John Betjeman from *Collected Poems*.

New Directions Publishing Corporation: 'October' by Denise Levertov from *Poems 1960–1967*. Copyright © 1964 by Denise Levertov Goodman.

Penguin Books Ltd.: 'The Cowherd' by Lu Yen and 'The Fortune-teller' by Chu Tun-ju from *The Penguin Book of Chinese Verse* translations by Robert Kotewell and Norman L. Smith (The Penguin Books, 1962), translation copyright © N. L. Smith and R. H. Kotewell 1962.

A. D. Peters & Co. Ltd.: '40–Love' by Roger McGough from *After the Merrymaking* (USA). Extract from *The Dynamics of Creation* by Dr Anthony Storr.

Random House Inc.: 'The Pylons' by Stephen Spender. © 1934 and renewed 1962 by Stephen Spender. Reprinted from *Selected Poems* by Stephen Spender by permission of Random House Inc. (world excluding UK and British Commonwealth).

Routledge & Kegan Paul Plc.: 'Witches Song' by B. Jonson.

George Sassoon: 'Idyll' by Siegfried Sassoon.

A. P. Watt Ltd.: 'Brother' and 'Traveller's Curse after Misdirection' by Robert Graves from *Collected Poems 1975* and *Collected Poems 1965* respectively. Reprinted by permission of A. P. Watt Ltd. on behalf of the Executors of the Estate of Robert Graves.

Every effort has been made to trace and acknowledge copyright owners. If any right has been omitted the publishers offer their apologies and will rectify this in subsequent editions following notification.